*Historic walks
in Sherwood Forest*

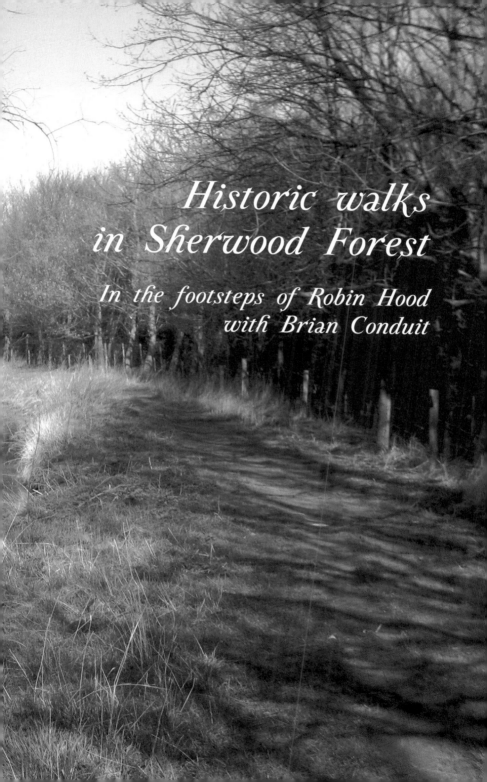

Historic walks in Sherwood Forest

In the footsteps of Robin Hood
with Brian Conduit

First published in 2012
by Palatine Books,
Carnegie House,
Chatsworth Road
Lancaster LA1 4SL
www.carnegiepublishing.com

British Library Cataloguing-in-Publication data
A catalogue record for this book is available from the British Library

Printed and bound in the UK by Henry Ling Ltd

ISBN: 978 1 874181-83-5

Contents

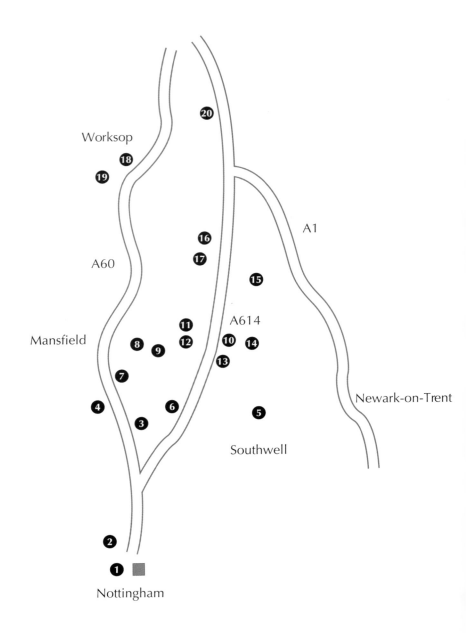

Introduction

'I have been in the back woods of the American continent, and seen many noble 'green-robed senators' of the forest in England, but I never knew what a tree was until I beheld the giants of Sherwood.'

J. Searle, Victorian writer

History of Sherwood Forest

Sherwood literally means 'shire wood', the wood of the shire of Nottingham, and in medieval times was a vast expanse of thick woodland and open heathland about 25 miles long and between 8 and 10 miles wide. The forest stretched from Nottingham in the south almost to Worksop in the north, and from the fringes of the Peak District in the west to the Trent Valley in the east.

It was one of around 90 royal forests scattered throughout England. Although most people think of a forest as mainly comprising well-wooded country, in medieval England a royal forest was any piece of land in which the king had sole hunting rights, and was more of a legal and administrative than a physical or geographical term. In Sherwood and the other royal forests the king's hunting rights were maintained by a harsh set of laws, enforced by a vast bureaucracy of foresters, forest courts and judges. Punishments for those who broke the forest laws were severe – loss of life or limb for the serious offence of poaching the king's deer and a heavy fine or imprisonment for the less serious offences of felling a tree or making clearances in the forest. People could even be hauled before the forest courts for stealing a branch to use for firewood.

These laws were hated by people from all walks of life who lived within the royal forests. A landowner was not allowed to chop down his own trees or create more space for growing crops on his own land without the permission of the royal foresters, and a peasant who saw a herd of deer trampling all over his crops could only look on helplessly as his family faced possible starvation. In these circumstances it is not surprising that outlaws who sought refuge in the forests and successfully defied the forest laws by living off the king's deer became admirable heroes, perhaps the likeliest origin for the Robin Hood legends.

Although the laws were widely disliked, the royal forests were popular with most medieval monarchs and Sherwood was particularly favoured as it was conveniently close to the royal castle at Nottingham. Around the middle of the twelfth century Henry II built a hunting lodge in the heart of the forest at Clipstone, although it has become known as King John's Palace, the name of one of his sons. In 1194 Richard the Lionheart entertained the King of Scotland there and documents record that 'Clipstone and the forest of Sherwood pleased him much.' Not far from Clipstone stand the remains of an ancient oak under whose branches Edward I is alleged to have held a meeting of Parliament in 1290, hence its name the Parliament Oak.

At their height in the thirteenth century the royal forests covered about a third of the entire country but in the later Middle Ages they gradually decreased in size, and the forest laws became less onerous and were less rigidly enforced. Throughout the fourteenth and fifteenth centuries kings were almost permanently short of money, largely as a result of the high cost of waging wars against France and Scotland, and one way of raising revenue was to sell-off blocks of forest land. Another way was to punish infringements of the forest laws by fines instead of imprisonment or mutilation.

The selling-off of royal forest land in Sherwood and elsewhere accelerated from the sixteenth century onwards. Tudor and Stuart monarchs were less interested in hunting than their medieval predecessors and the forest laws were allowed to lapse and in time became obsolete. Over the following centuries many of the landowners who had acquired new estates in the former royal forests carved out landscaped parklands and built grand houses for themselves. Four of these great parklands in the northern part of Sherwood – Worksop, Welbeck, Clumber and Thoresby – were owned at one time or another by ducal families, hence their nickname 'Dukeries'.

In the Dukeries and on other estates the decline of the forest was partially arrested by the wholesale planting of new woodlands, but in the remainder of Sherwood the sixteenth to nineteenth centuries was a period of continuous destruction. Thousands of famed Sherwood oaks were felled to meet the demands of the navy and iron industry and to make way for the further encroachments of agriculture. In the early eighteenth century Daniel Defoe wrote: 'If there was such a man as Robin Hood, he would hardly find shelter for a week.'

In the nineteenth century railways opened up hitherto remote and unknown parts of Sherwood and the first coal mines appeared on the fringes of the forest. Destruction of the Sherwood woodlands reached its peak in the First World War when there was an urgent need for timber, but the deficiencies in the nation's timber supplies revealed by the war led to the turning of the tide. In 1919 the Forestry Commission was set up and early in the 1920s began replanting large parts of the old forest with conifers – chiefly Corsican and Scots pine. Some further damage to the forest occurred in the Second World War when it was used as an ammunition dump and for tank training purposes, but since then there has been a change of attitude with more emphasis on tourism, promoting greater public access to the woodlands and conserving what is left of the older parts of the forest.

Nowadays most of the conifer woods are open to the public and much of the traditional oak and birch forest and many of the landscaped parklands have come into the ownership of public authorities – English Nature, National Trust, and Nottinghamshire County Council – who encourage visitors by providing car parks, information centres and refreshment facilities. As most of the coal mines have now gone, tourism has become an important part of the economy of this part of Nottinghamshire, and, with its attractive mixture of woodland, parkland and heath, plus miles of well-signed public footpaths, walkers are increasingly attracted to Sherwood Forest.

Of course there is one aspect of the forest's heritage that both walkers and other visitors to the area will be aware of wherever they go, the unseen but powerful presence of its most famous hero.

Robin Hood

Did he really exist? Millions of words have been spoken and written on this thorny and controversial subject, and a wide variety of scholars – from university academics to groups of amateur local historians – have studied and investigated it at length but have failed to come up with any conclusive answer. Today Robin Hood remains just as elusive a figure to us as he was in the Middle Ages to his great adversary, the notorious Sheriff of Nottingham.

What can we be sure of? Firstly Robin Hood was not an uncommon Christian and surname combination in medieval England. Secondly there were many outlaws at the time in Sherwood and other English forests. Thirdly there were Sheriffs of Nottingham (actually of Nottinghamshire and Derbyshire) throughout the Middle Ages. Fourthly medieval kings frequently visited Sherwood on hunting expeditions. Finally, stories about Robin Hood were in existence as early as the fourteenth or even the thirteenth century.

The main problem is that Robin Hood cannot be identified with any historical figure of flesh and blood, or with any precise historical event. Some of the legends and ballads associate him with Richard I and his brother Prince John in the late twelfth and early thirteenth centuries, while others place him at a later date during the reign of a King Edward. However, unfortunately there were three King Edwards between 1272 and 1377. No specific king, no real life bishop, abbot or baron and no particular sheriff are ever mentioned.

Paradoxically, even though the legends about when Robin Hood actually lived are vague, they are far more specific about *where* he lived. All the stories place him firmly in the forests of Sherwood and the lesser known Barnsdale, an area that extends through Nottinghamshire and South Yorkshire – roughly from Nottingham to Doncaster and Wakefield. Even this is controversial as the earliest legends refer more often to Barnsdale Forest than the more familiar Sherwood. Many people will never have heard of Barnsdale and probably even fewer have any idea of where it is. Unlike Sherwood it was never a royal forest but a small, thickly-wooded area to the north of Doncaster which has now largely disappeared. Over the centuries both forests have claimed to be the real home of the heroic outlaw chief. Was he a Nottinghamshire or a Yorkshire man?

The truth is that he probably belonged to both. On its own Barnsdale covered too small an area to have offered refuge to a band of outlaws for long and it is likely that in the Middle Ages the two forests were virtually adjacent and formed one large well-wooded tract of land. It is noteworthy that the recently opened airport near Doncaster has been named after Robin Hood in recognition of his association with that part of South Yorkshire.

Although we may not be able to identify him with any historical figure or precise event, the legends were in existence by the late fourteenth century. The earliest reference to them is in William Langland's *Piers Plowman*, which appeared around 1377, but Robin Hood's name crops up even earlier in court records from 1261. The original stories of his exploits are based on a few surviving medieval legends – *Robin Hood and the Monk, Robin Hood and the Potter* and *A Lyttell Geste of Robyn Hode*. Some of the main characters – Little John, the Sheriff of Nottingham and Guy of Gisborne – are present in the early stories but Maid Marian and Friar Tuck do not appear until later, in the sixteenth century.

By the end of the fifteenth century Robin Hood's fame had spread far and wide, even across the Scottish border, and he was a frequent character in May Day festivities and dramatic productions. By then other outlaws and rebels were calling themselves Robin Hood or were accused of acting in the manner of him – robbing the rich to give to the poor – just like later lawless characters in other parts of the world, such as Jesse James in the American West and Ned Kelly in Australia. With the onset of mass travel in the nineteenth century, places associated with Robin Hood in Sherwood Forest and elsewhere in the locality, such as Little John's Grave at Hathersage in Derbyshire, Edwinstowe Church (alleged setting for the marriage of Robin and Maid Marian) and particularly the Major Oak, became popular tourist attractions.

One plausible theory is that perhaps there was more than one Robin Hood. He may be a composite figure based on several real outlaws who over the centuries have become fused into one folk hero, a symbol of the fight against injustice and tyranny who always stood up for the downtrodden and dispossessed. Over the years as his brave and daring exploits were passed down from hand to mouth, they were added to, altered and inevitably exaggerated.

In more recent times, novels, Hollywood movies and television series have only added to the myth.

It is interesting that throughout the centuries, the stories of Robin Hood have been interpreted in a variety of ways according to the contemporary beliefs and attitudes. Sometimes he has been thought of as a yeoman and other times identified as a nobleman, the Earl of Huntingdon. Victorian novels depicted him as a patriotic hero, like those contemporary heroes who at the time were carrying out daring deeds in the jungles of Africa or the outback of Australia. He has been a social reformer, philanthropist or a rebel. At one time he was even banned in some of the American states because his habit of trying to redistribute wealth by robbing from the rich in order to feed the poor smacked too much of Communism! Robin Hood can be all things to all men, perhaps a major reason for his continuing popularity over the centuries.

His exploits make excellent adventure stories and have stood the test of time. Despite competition from later heroes– such as Superman, Batman and Spiderman – who all possessed far more hi-tech equipment than a bow and arrow, this Nottinghamshire outlaw is still as popular as ever.

The supply of new films and television series seems to be inexhaustible and will probably continue forever, or at least for a long time to come.

The legend of Robin Hood makes a visit to Sherwood Forest all the more enjoyable and interesting. It is an attractive walking area in its own right but the outlaw hero just adds that extra unseen pleasure and excitement when strolling through the thick woodland and across the open heath and grassland of the forest. Sherwood is waiting to be explored, much smaller than it was in the Middle Ages but still in the twenty-first century an authentic example of the traditional English greenwood.

General Information

Useful Organisations

The Ramblers' Association, 2nd Floor, Camelford House, 87–90 Albert Embankment, London SE1 7TW
Tel: 020 7339 8500 Email: ramblers@ramblers.org.uk

The National Trust, Heelis Building, Kemble Drive, Swindon, Wiltshire, SN2 2NA
Tel: 01793 817400 Email: enquiries@nationaltrust.org.uk

East Midlands Regional Office, Clumber Park Stableyard, Worksop, Nottinghamshire, S80 3BE
Tel: 01909 486411 Email: enquiries@nationaltrust.org.uk

Public Transport

For information about bus services and timetables contact Traveline either by visiting www.traveline.org.uk or phoning 0871 200 2233. Alternatively contact the local tourist information centre.

Maps

The sketch maps used in this book are only a rough guide and you should always take with you the relevant Ordnance Survey map. The best maps for walkers are the Explorer maps and fortunately the vast majority of the walks are covered by Explorer 270 (Sherwood Forest). Two of the walks require Explorer 260 (Nottingham), two need Explorer 271 (Newark-on-Trent) and one is covered by Explorer 279 (Doncaster).

Tourist Information

For information about Sherwood Forest and the adjoining area visit the Nottinghamshire tourist information website at www.experiencenottinghamshire.com or contact the local visitor information centres. Phone numbers and email addresses are given below.

Newark 01636 655765 newarktic@nsdc.info
Nottingham 08444 775678 tourist.information@nottinghamcity.gov.uk
Retford 01777 860780 retford.tourist@bassetlaw.gov.uk
Sherwood (Ollerton Heath) 01623 824545 ollerton@nsdc.info
Sherwood Forest Visitor Centre (Edwinstowe) 01623 823202 enquiries@nottscc.gov.uk
Southwell 01636 655765 southwelltourism@btconnect.com
Worksop 01909 501148 worksop.tourist@bassetlaw.gov.uk

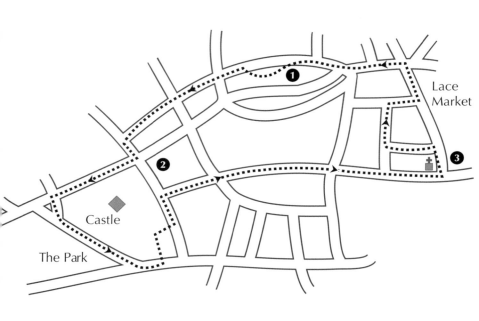

Lace
Market

1

2

3

Castle

The Park

Nottingham: A City Walk

LENGTH:	1 ¾ miles (2.8 km)
TIME:	1 ¼ hours
TERRAIN:	Easy town walking
START/PARKING:	Nottingham, Old Market Square, GR SK573399. Car parks in Nottingham or alternatively use the Park and Ride scheme
PUBLIC TRANSPORT:	Nottingham is easily reached by train and bus from all the local towns
REFRESHMENTS:	Plenty of restaurants, wine bars, pubs and cafés in Nottingham
MAP:	OS Explorer 260 – Nottingham, or pick up a street map from the tourist information centre

ℹ Nottingham has always been the southern gateway to Sherwood Forest and in the Middle Ages the forest actually extended right up to the walls of its royal castle. In the Robin Hood legends it is obviously most famous as the headquarters of the sheriff, the outlaw chief's most persistent enemy. Although the walk is a short one, there is much to see and it is packed with interest and variety which makes the estimated time of 1 ¼ hours rather meaningless, based purely on walking time only. The route takes in the castle, sites associated with the English Civil War, part of a planned nineteenth-century estate, the oldest inn in England (allegedly), historic churches, and the monumental Victorian warehouses of the Lace Market, formerly the hub of the city's most distinctive industry.

● **Start in the Old Market Square and with your back to the Council House, walk across the square to the far side and continue along St James's Street. Cross the dual carriageway (Maid Marian Way) and keep along St James's Street until you reach a T-junction.**

ℹ There are two interesting wall plaques around here. The first is on a house to your right which states that for a short period in 1798-99 this was the home of Lord Byron. Just after turning left at the T-junction another plaque indicates that near here Charles I raised his standard on 22 August 1642, a gesture that marked the official start of the English Civil War.

Turn left into St James's Terrace and continue down Standard Hill to the gatehouse of Nottingham Castle.

ABOVE: OLD MARKET SQUARE, NOTTINGHAM

OPPOSITE: GATEHOUSE OF NOTTINGHAM CASTLE

❶ Of the great medieval royal fortress virtually nothing remains except for the heavily restored gatehouse and some of the outer walls. The present castle is chiefly a seventeenth-century palace, built by the Duke of Newcastle soon after its predecessor was destroyed after the Civil War. Even this was gutted by fire during the Reform Bill riots of 1831, but it was later restored and reopened in 1878 by the Prince of Wales as a municipal art gallery and museum. Passages lead from the castle down through the sandstone rock on which it stands to ground level, and one of them, Mortimer's Hole, is allegedly the route by which agents of Edward III gained access to the castle in 1330 in order to capture Queen Isabella – wife of the brutally murdered Edward II – and Roger Mortimer, her lover and co-conspirator in her husband's death.

❷ **The next part of the route is a circuit of the base of the Castle Rock. The chief reasons for this short detour is that it takes you into a small area of The Park Estate and it enables you to view the Castle Rock from a variety of angles and to see the many caves carved out of it.**

ⓘ The nineteenth-century Park Estate occupies the royal park that in the Middle Ages adjoined Nottingham Castle and as such was part of Sherwood Forest. When the castle became the property of the Duke of Newcastle, it changed from a royal to a ducal park. It remained as parkland until the second half of the nineteenth century when it was developed as an exclusive residential area for the 'lace barons' and other industrial tycoons of Nottingham and the surrounding area. It is fine example of Victorian town planning, with large villas surrounded by spacious gardens and laid out in a series of drives, circuses and crescents. The walk only embraces a very small part of it.

⊛ **At the castle entrance turn right along Lenton Road to enter The Park and take the first road on the left (Ogle Drive). Bear left along Peveril Drive to leave the estate and turn left into Castle Boulevard. Before reaching traffic lights, turn left through gates and walk along a path across a small grassy area towards the Castle Rock. Follow the path to the right, passing Ye Olde Trip to Jerusalem Inn, to emerge onto Castle Road.**

ⓘ At the base of the Castle Rock is Brewhouse Yard where a group of seventeenth-century cottages house the Museum of Nottingham

Life. This tells the social history of Nottingham over the last 300 years.

Adjacent to it is the famous Trip to Jerusalem, a must for any visitor to the city. This fascinating old pub claims to be the oldest in England, dating back to 1189. In the Middle Ages the word 'trip' meant a stopping or resting place on a journey rather than the journey itself, and allegedly the pub originated as a place where soldiers joining the Third Crusade rested on their way to the Holy Land. It is a most atmospheric place to stop for a drink – as much a museum as a pub – and several of its rooms are caves carved out of the Castle Rock.

Turn left up Castle Road following the line of the castle walls and soon you will see to your left the statue of Robin Hood, just below the gatehouse and on the site of the castle moat. As well as the statue, there are a series of plaques

OPPOSITE: THE SANDSTONE ROCK ON WHICH NOTTINGHAM CASTLE STANDS IS HONEYCOMBED WITH CAVES

ABOVE: YE OLDE TRIP TO JERUSALEM INN AT THE BASE OF THE CASTLE ROCK

depicting episodes in the life of the outlaw hero. Opposite the statue turn right into the pedestrianised Castle Gate. From here to St Mary's Church you follow a Robin Hood Trail with plenty of information boards at intervals.

ⓘ On the corner of Castle Road and Castle Gate is a half-timbered building called Severns. Re-erected here from another site, it is a fine example of a fourteenth-century town house. It now houses the Lace Centre, which details the history of the lace industry and has a shop where you can buy lace products.

After recrossing Maid Marian Way, St Nicholas's Church is seen over to the right. During the Civil War its tower was used by Royalist troops to bombard the castle, which at the time was occupied by Parliamentary forces, for five days in September 1643. As a result the commander of the castle garrison ordered it to be demolished to prevent a repetition but the church was rebuilt later in the seventeenth century. On the left are two more of Nottingham's old pubs, the Royal Children and the Salutation, the latter only a few years younger than the Trip to Jerusalem.

⚲   **Keep ahead along Castle Gate and at the next crossroads continue gently uphill along Low Pavement and Middle Pavement to Weekday Cross. Continue along High Pavement towards St Mary's Church, here entering the Lace Market.**

ABOVE: STATUE OF ROBIN HOOD IN CHARACTERISTIC POSE

❶ On the right you pass the handsome eighteenth-century Shire Hall, now the Galleries of Justice Museum which depicts the history of crime and punishment. To the left is the imposing St Mary's Church, a grand example of a mainly fifteenth-century town church.

In the second half of the nineteenth century the Lace Market became the manufacturing and commercial centre of the lace industry and is dominated by a number of ornate and monumental warehouses. At the time the lace industry flourished because of the Victorian mania for lace products – curtains, tablecloths, handkerchiefs etc. – and the vast majority of these were made in Nottingham. On the following brief tour of the Lace Market, some of the most impressive of the former Victorian lace warehouses (mostly built between 1845 and 1865) are seen.

❸ Just beyond St Mary's Church turn left into Stoney Street and left again into Broadway. Follow the road between towering warehouses to a T-junction and turn right; when you reach another, turn right again. You will then arrive at a third T-junction, where you should turn left, here rejoining Stoney Street. Turn left along Carlton Street and at a fork take the right-hand pedestrianised street (Pelham Street) which leads back into the Old Market Square.

ABOVE: GRAND VICTORIAN FORMER WAREHOUSES IN THE LACE MARKET

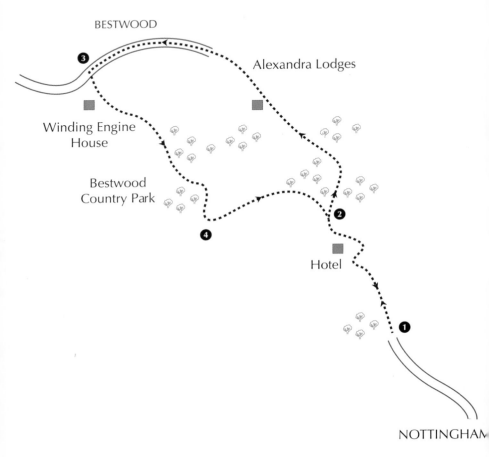

BESTWOOD

Alexandra Lodges

Winding Engine
House

Bestwood
Country Park

Hotel

NOTTINGHAM

Bestwood Country Park

LENGTH:	3 ½ miles (5.6 km)
TIME:	2 hours
TERRAIN:	Mainly well-surfaced woodland tracks and paths, one stretch of quiet lane, some modest climbing
START/PARKING:	Bestwood Country Park, signposted from the A60 on the northern edge of Nottingham, car park at the end of Bestwood Lodge Drive, GR SK572465
PUBLIC TRANSPORT:	Buses from Nottingham to Bestwood Lodge Drive, then about a 15-minute walk to the starting point
REFRESHMENTS:	None
MAP:	OS Explorer 260 – Nottingham

Bestwood has had a varied history and you see plenty of reminders of its past on this walk. Most of the route is either through or along the edge of the attractive woodlands of the country park, located on the northern fringes of Nottingham, which is the nearest remnant of Sherwood Forest to the city. There are a few gradients but these are all easy and gradual.

ℹ Medieval forest, ducal parkland, site of a colliery and now a popular recreation area: this is the rough chronological list of the various roles of Bestwood Park throughout its long history. Now covering an area of 650 acres, it was originally a hunting area of nearly 4,000 acres, the most southerly part of the medieval royal forest. In the seventeenth century the park was enclosed from open forest land and in 1683.

ℹ In the seventeenth century the park was enclosed from open forest land and in 1683 Charles II gave it to his illegitimate son by Nell Gwynn, who the king made 1st Duke of St Albans. The most dramatic changes to the park were made by the 10th Duke during the second half of the nineteenth century. He pulled down the

ABOVE: WOODLAND IN BESTWOOD COUNTRY PARK, THE MOST SOUTHERLY REMNANT OF SHERWOOD FOREST

OPPOSITE: ALEXANDRA LODGE, BUILT IN 1871 AS A GATEHOUSE TO BESTWOOD PARK

old hunting lodge and built the present imposing Victorian house, now a hotel, between 1858 and 1863. A few years later in 1871 he built Alexandra Lodge as a gatehouse to the park. He was also responsible for the development of Bestwood Colliery and the adjoining mining village. In 1939 the park was requisitioned by the army and it became a country park in the 1970s.

❶ Turn right out of the car park and head gently uphill along a tarmac drive through woodland to the car park adjoining Bestwood Lodge. Do not bear left into the hotel car park but turn sharp right to continue along the main drive.

❷ At a three-way fork, continue along the right-hand drive, signposted to Alexandra Lodges, and at the next fork, take the left-hand drive (still in the Alexandra Lodges direction). Go through a kissing gate and head gently downhill, passing through the archway of the redbrick Victorian lodge. Keep ahead along the tarmac track (it later becomes a lane) which curves gently to the left along the edge of Bestwood, a former mining village.

❸ Look out for where you turn left along a tarmac drive to Bestwood Country Park car park. Do not bear left into the car park but keep ahead through a kissing gate to Bestwood Colliery Winding Engine House.

ⓘ Bestwood Colliery was developed in the 1870s and at its height employed 1,300 people. Mining ceased in 1967 and all that remains of it is the Winding Engine House and nearby Dynamo House, recently restored as a visitor attraction and an impressive legacy of its previous history.

Take the path that passes to the left of the Winding Engine House and Dynamo House, and at a fork, take the left-hand path – signposted to Alexandra Lodges and Big Wood – which curves gradually right along the edge of woodland.

At a junction of paths, keep ahead, in Big Wood direction, now re-entering woodland, and at the next fork, continue along the right-hand path, signposted to Big Wood and Lodge Gardens. At another fork immediately ahead, take the

right-hand wider path which heads steadily uphill through the trees, curving gradually to the left to reach a T-junction at the top of a ridge.

❹ Turn left and walk along the ridge – there are lots of forks but take the right-hand path every time, keeping close to the right inside edge of the wooded park. Eventually the path curves gradually right and heads downhill to a kissing gate. **❷** Go through onto the main drive again, here rejoining the outward route, and retrace your steps past the hotel down to the start.

ABOVE AND OPPOSITE: THE WINDING ENGINE HOUSE OF THE FORMER BESTWOOD COLLIERY

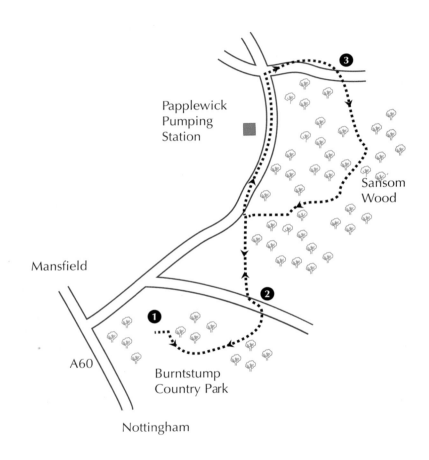

Papplewick
Pumping
Station

Sansom
Wood

Mansfield

A60

Burntstump
Country Park

Nottingham

Burntstump Country Park and Sansom Wood

LENGTH:	4 miles (6.4 km)
TIME:	2 hours
TERRAIN:	Woodland paths and tracks, one stretch along a lane
START/PARKING:	Burntstump Country Park, situated just to the east of the A60 between Nottingham and Mansfield, GR SK575505
PUBLIC TRANSPORT:	Buses from Nottingham and Mansfield stop nearby
REFRESHMENTS:	Pub by the country park
MAP:	OS Explorer 270 – Sherwood Forest

Burntstump Country Park and Sansom Wood are virtually adjacent; the former is a remnant of Sherwood Forest and the latter is a more recent Forestry Commission plantation. The first part of the walk is through woodland on the top edge of the country park before descending to a lane and passing Papplewick Pumping Station. This is followed by an attractive circuit of part of Sansom Wood before retracing your steps to the start.

ⓘ Burntstump Country Park is a piece of old Sherwood, situated just a few miles north of Nottingham, that has managed to survive amidst agricultural encroachment, urban spread and industrial development. Some ancient gnarled oaks, reminiscent of parts of Birklands, can still be seen here. It comprises an arc of sloping woodland that almost encloses an area of grassland which includes a cricket pitch. Given its proximity to the city it is not surprising that it is a popular weekend and bank holiday venue, with plenty of woodland walks, open grassland and a pub.

❶ At the far end of the car park by the toilet block, turn right along an uphill path to a track where you turn left into woodland, here joining the Robin Hood Way. Keep on the main track all the while, heading gently uphill and curving gradually left to a gate. Pass beside it and keep ahead along a tarmac track, curving left to reach a road.

ABOVE: OVERLOOKING THE CRICKET FIELD AT BURNTSTUMP COUNTRY PARK

OPPOSITE: PAPPLEWICK PUMPING STATION

❷ **Turn left – there is a path on the right-hand side of the road – take the first turning on the right and continue gently downhill along the left edge of Sansom Wood until you reach a lane. Keep ahead, still by the left edge of the wood, passing the entrance to Papplewick Pumping Station.**

ⓘ Although a spectacular example of Victorian engineering, the ornate Papplewick Pumping Station is as much a triumph of Victorian architecture and craftsmanship. It was opened in 1884 to supplement the water supply of the fast expanding city of Nottingham. Described as the finest working pumping station in the country, it comprises an Engine House (which houses two massive and original Watt beam engines), Boiler House and Cooling Pond all set in attractively landscaped grounds. There is also a shop and café. Opening times are limited mainly to certain Sundays and Bank Holidays throughout the year; you can obtain details of these times and when steaming events are taking place either by phoning 0115 963 2938 or visiting www.papplewickpumpingstation.co.uk

Keep ahead to a crossroads and turn right. You can continue along this road for just over ¼ mile (400 m) but a pleasanter alternative is to turn left onto a narrow path into the trees – this is at a small layby just where the road bears slightly right – and turn sharp right on meeting a track which bends left and keeps parallel to the road.

❸ Cross over where you see a Forestry Commission sign for Sansom Wood on the opposite side of the road, pass beside a barrier and take the clear path through the wood.

❶ Much of the old Sansom Wood was felled in the seventeenth and eighteenth centuries to serve the local iron industries. The present wood was acquired by the Forestry Commission in 1973 and forms part of the large block of woodland around Blidworth. Although mainly coniferous, comprising pine and larch, it still retains some of its traditional broadleaved trees, including birch, beech, sycamore and sweet chestnut, and makes an attractive walking area.

Cross a bridge over a disused railway track and keep ahead on the main path at all junctions, heading gently uphill to reach a T-junction on the brow of a low hill. Turn right and the track curves gradually left to another junction of paths and tracks. Follow the main track to the right, heading gently downhill, and pass beside a barrier onto a lane. Turn left, here rejoining the outward route, and retrace your steps to the start.

ABOVE: THE FINAL DESCENT TO THE CAR PARK

OPPOSITE: THE PUMPING STATION CHIMNEY IS A MAJOR LANDMARK

In the footsteps of Robin Hood   19

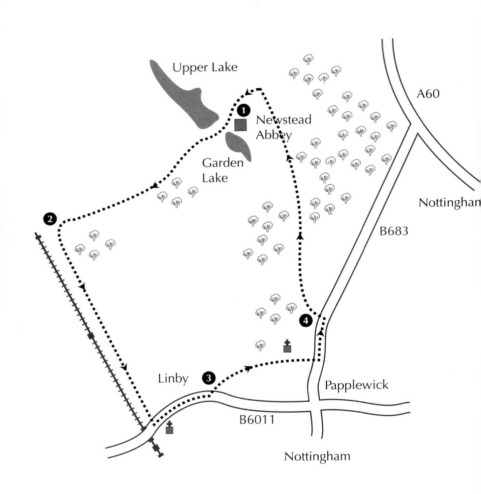

Upper Lake

1 Newstead Abbey

Garden Lake

A60

Nottingham

B683

2

4

Linby 3

Papplewick

B6011

Nottingham

Newstead Abbey, Linby and Papplewick

4

LENGTH:	6 miles (9.7 km)
TIME:	3 hours
TERRAIN:	Field paths, woodland tracks and one stretch along a disused railway line
START/PARKING:	Newstead Abbey, off A60 between Nottingham and Mansfield, GR SK541539
PUBLIC TRANSPORT:	Buses from Nottingham and Mansfield stop at the entrance to Newstead Abbey, from there a walk of about 1 mile (1.6 km) along the drive brings you to the starting point.
REFRESHMENTS:	Café at Newstead Abbey, pub at Linby, pub at Papplewick
MAP:	OS Explorer 270 – Sherwood Forest

The first part of the walk is beside the lake and through the trees of Newstead Park, originally part of Sherwood Forest. It continues along a disused railway track to the attractive village of Linby and then via field paths to the neighbouring village of Papplewick. A tree-lined track, once a major route through the medieval forest, returns you to the start and from this track there are fine and extensive views over the park and surrounding countryside.

❶ **From the car park, head down the tarmac drive to the house and lake.**

ⓘ 'A monarch bade thee from that wild arise, Where Sherwood's outlaws once were wont to prowl.' This is how one of its later owners, the poet Lord Byron, described the origins of Newstead Abbey. It was founded as an Augustinian priory around 1170 by Henry II as part of his atonement to the church for the murder of Thomas Becket, Archbishop of Canterbury. All that remains of this medieval priory is the impressive thirteenth-century west front of the church. After the dissolution of the monasteries in the 1530s, the monastic estates were bought by Sir John Byron and he and his successors converted the priory into a fine country house, renamed Newstead Abbey. Despite later alterations and additions, the house still retains a distinct monastic atmosphere as parts of the medieval priory have been incorporated into its structure.

The Byrons were a colourful family. The 5th Lord killed one of his neighbours during a drunken duel in a London tavern, though he was acquitted of the murder. He was responsible for the landscaping of the grounds in the eighteenth century and also built the two medieval-looking forts on the side of the Upper Lake. These were used during the staging of mock sea battles on

ABOVE AND OPPOSITE: MOCK FORTS OVERLOOKING THE UPPER LAKE AT NEWSTEAD ABBEY

the lake, a legacy of his previous career as a naval officer. Such extravagances bankrupted him which meant that when the 6th Lord, the famous poet, inherited the estate in 1798, the house was in a very dilapidated state and there were huge debts. He was a notorious gambler and womaniser and although he loved Newstead, his private life piled up more debts and prevented him from ever being able to raise the money to restore the house. He was forced to sell it in 1817 and died in 1824 at the early age of 36, while helping the Greeks in their war of independence against the Turks. The estate was purchased by Colonel Wildman and he had the money to carry out a thorough renovation and restoration, and the present appearance of Newstead Abbey is mainly the result of his efforts. After several later owners, the house and park were eventually given to the City of Nottingham in 1931. The house contains much Byron memorabilia – letters, furniture, paintings – and is surrounded by attractive formal gardens. While walking around the gardens, make sure that you look out for the monument to Boatswain, the poet's dog.

Follow the drive as it curves right between the Upper and Garden Lakes and later continues through trees. After 1 ¼ miles (2 km), you pass between gateposts and beside a barrier to a junction of paths and tracks. Bear left along an enclosed path, signposted to Nottingham and Hucknall, until reaching a T-junction.

❷ Turn left onto a tree-lined track to join the Linby Trail, part of a cycleway between Nottingham and Worksop. This stretch uses the track of a former railway. Keep ahead at a crossways and after passing beside a barrier, the route continues through more open country. Eventually you pass beside a gate and should keep ahead to emerge onto a road. Then turn left into Linby.

ⓘ Most Nottinghamshire villages are built of brick but Linby and the neighbouring village of Papplewick are rare examples of stone-built villages. The stone is the creamy-coloured local limestone. With its main street lined by streams on both sides, medieval church and ancient crosses at each end, Linby is often considered to be the most attractive village in the county. The church contains some Norman

work and has a fifteenth-century tower. In the churchyard the unmarked graves of 163 pauper children are a stark reminder of the harsh conditions in the nearby textile mills of the Leen Valley during the early years of the Industrial Revolution. Of the two crosses, the second one at the far end of the village is said to mark the boundary of medieval Sherwood. Another link with the forest is that in the Middle Ages Linby was one of the meeting places for the forest courts, held there every six weeks on a Monday.

Walk through the village and on along Linby Lane.

ABOVE AND OPPOSITE: THE PICTURESQUE VILLAGE OF LINBY

❸ Just before the road bears right, turn left beside a gate, at a public footpath sign, and walk along the left edge of a field. Keep ahead through a belt of trees, cross a footbridge over the little River Leen, go through a gate and continue along the left edge of the next field. Over to the left the tower of Papplewick Church can be seen through the trees. Go through a gate onto a tarmac drive and a short detour to the left brings you into the churchyard.

ⓘ A huge ancient yew tree dominates Papplewick churchyard. Apart from the fourteenth-century tower, the church was rebuilt in the eighteenth century by Frederick Montagu, owner of Papplewick Hall. Inside on the floor of the nave is a monument of a forester, showing his bow and arrow, belt and hunting horn. The eighteenth-century hall, seen shortly on the walk, is thought to have been designed by the renowned Adam brothers.

ABOVE: THIS TRACK NEAR NEWSTEAD ABBEY WAS A MEDIEVAL ROUTEWAY THROUGH THE FOREST

OPPOSITE: THE THIRTEENTH CENTURY WEST FRONT OF THE MEDIEVAL PRIORY AT NEWSTEAD ADJOINS THE LATER HOUSE

The route continues to the right along the tarmac drive. Pass between gates and keep ahead to emerge onto a road at the top of the main street in Papplewick. Turn right for the village and pub; otherwise turn left along the road and follow it around right and left bends. Papplewick Hall can be seen over to the left.

❹ At the next right bend, turn left along a track (Hall Lane) at a public footpath sign to Newstead Abbey and Larch Farm. The rest of the walk follows the chief route in medieval times through Sherwood Forest between Nottingham and Mansfield.

Where the main track bends left, keep ahead beside a gate, continue along a track and after going through a gate, the track narrows to a woodland path. Bear left on joining a straight tarmac track and look out for where it curves slightly left. At this point, bear right onto a narrow path – there is a public footpath post just ahead – which winds through trees to reach the main drive of Newstead Abbey. Then turn left for the short distance back to the start.

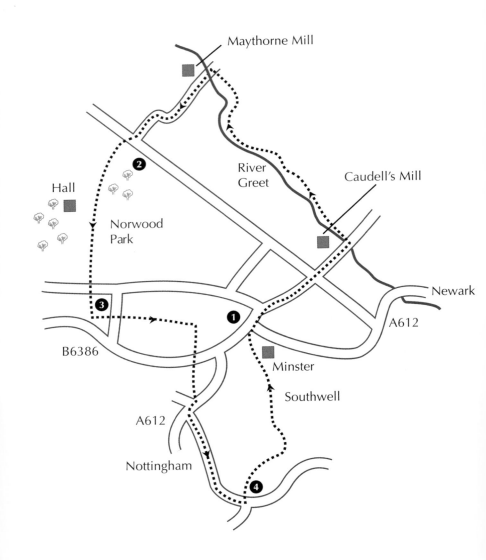

Southwell, River Greet and Norwood Park

5

LENGTH:	5 ½ miles (8.9 km)
TIME:	3 hours
TERRAIN:	Easy walking on well-signed tracks and field paths, one modest climb
START/PARKING:	Southwell, road junction in town centre by the Saracen's Head, GR SK701539. Car parks at Southwell
PUBLIC TRANSPORT:	Buses from Nottingham, Mansfield and Newark
REFRESHMENTS:	Pubs and cafés at Southwell
MAPS:	OS Explorers 270 – Sherwood Forest and 271 – Newark-on-Trent

Southwell is situated near the eastern edge of medieval Sherwood and this walk falls into three parts. First comes a delightful ramble across meadows along the banks of the meandering River Greet. Next is a walk through Norwood Park, with views of the eighteenth-century hall, and after that you climb gently onto a low hill. On the final descent into Southwell there are extensive views across the Trent Valley and over the town below, dominated by its beautiful minster. Leave plenty of time to explore this fascinating little town, especially the superb and intricate carvings in the Chapter House of the minster, thought to have been inspired by the proximity of Sherwood Forest.

1 The pleasant, quiet little town of Southwell, situated between the eastern edge of Sherwood Forest and the Trent Valley, possesses what is possibly England's least known but at the same time one of its most beautiful cathedrals. Southwell Minster was only raised to full cathedral status in 1884; during the Middle Ages it was a collegiate church and served as a sub-cathedral for the vast York diocese. Near the east end of the church the ruins of the medieval palace of the archbishops of York can be seen. Apart from the east end which was rebuilt in the thirteenth century, most of the minster dates from the early twelfth century and is a fine example of Norman architecture. The plain but dignified west front is distinguished by the short conical spires on the twin towers and the interior reveals a striking contrast between the heavy rounded arches of the Norman nave and the more slender and elegant Gothic arches at the east end. Southwell's gem is undoubtedly the thirteenth-century Chapter House in which there is a magnificent display of the most detailed and intricate (and in some cases, humorous) stone carvings of people and animals, and the leaves, flowers and berries of the local countryside. Some of the carvings depict the Green Man, a mythical character who may well have been the background for the Robin Hood stories. Whoever the unknown mason was, it is thought that he must have obtained much of his inspiration and knowledge from the terrain of Sherwood Forest, just a few miles away.

The Saracen's Head, where the walk begins, has played a role in one of the most significant episodes in British history. In 1646, following his defeat in the Civil War, Charles I spent his last night as a free man here before surrendering to the Scottish Army camped nearby at Newark on the following day. From then on he was a prisoner either of the Scots or Parliament until his execution nearly three years later in January 1649.

1 **Facing the Saracen's Head, turn right through the small Market Place and walk along King Street. At a fork take the left-hand road, head gently downhill across the middle of a large green, called Burgage, and continue along Station Road. Just beyond a former mill complex, turn left, at a public footpath sign, and walk across a parking area.**

ⓘ There are impressive former mill buildings at both ends of the riverside section of the walk. This one, Caudwell's Mill, was a corn mill, and since closure in the 1970s it has been converted into apartments. Where you leave the river, after about 1 ½ miles (2.4 km), you walk between the buildings of Maythorne Mill, a former textile mill built around 1785. It continued in production until World War II and was converted into housing in the 1980s.

Ⓚ **On the next part of the route you follow the many meanders of the little River Greet on the left, going round several sharp bends and crossing three footbridges. The third of these bridges is just in front of Maythorne Mill and after crossing it, follow a tarmac path between the mill buildings and continue along a lane to a road.**

ABOVE: MEADOWS BESIDE THE RIVER GREET

❷ Turn right and at a public footpath sign, turn left along the tarmac drive of Norwood Park. Keep along the main drive all the while, ignoring turns to the right, until you reach a crossways. To the right is a fine view of the façade of the house.

❶ In medieval times Norwood Park was a deer park owned by the archbishops of York as part of the Manor of Southwell. It later passed into private hands and the present house, built in the eighteenth century, is regarded as a masterpiece of Georgian architecture. It is now a country hotel, not open to the general public, and recently a golf course has been created in part of the parkland to add to its amenities.

(X) At the crossways bear slightly to the left off the tarmac drive, at a public footpath sign by a redundant stile, and continue across an orchard. Pass another redundant stile and keep ahead in a straight line to a road. Cross over, head gently uphill along the path ahead and on the far side of the field, turn left and continue along its right edge to emerge onto a road.

(X) ❸ Cross over and take the path opposite, which soon becomes enclosed. On reaching the base of a short flight of steps, turn right onto another enclosed path and head gently downhill to a road. Cross over and at the footpath sign opposite, continue along an enclosed tarmac path, cross a footbridge over a brook and keep ahead, descending steps to a lane.

Turn left to a road, turn right and take the first lane on the left, signposted to the free long-stay car park. Keep ahead

OPPOSITE: THE IMPOSING BUILDINGS OF CAUDWELL'S MILL, WHERE YOU JOIN THE RIVER GREET

ABOVE: NORWOOD PARK

gently uphill, at a fork continue along the left-hand uphill lane and follow it around a left bend.

❹ Just where the lane bends to the right, turn left through a gap in the hedge and walk across a field, making for a footpath post on the far side. From here you will see superb views of Southwell Minster and over the wide expanses of the Trent Valley as you descend into the town.

At the footpath post bear right across the next field and in the corner, turn left and head gently downhill along the

right field edge. Later the path becomes enclosed between a hedge on the right and the railings bordering a school playing field on the left. At the bottom turn right onto a tarmac track, follow it around a left bend, cross a footbridge over a brook and turn right across a small car park to a footpath post.

Continue along a tarmac path by the left edge of a field and where the path bears right, bear left across grass to a wall corner where you go up steps. Turn first right and then left along an enclosed path (the ruins of the archbishop's palace are to the left), go up some steps and walk along the south side of the minster. Continue along the path ahead, go through an archway onto a road and turn right to return to the start.

OPPOSITE: SOUTHWELL MINSTER, ONE OF ENGLAND'S MOST BEAUTIFUL AND LEAST KNOWN CATHEDRALS

ABOVE: SARACEN'S HEAD, WHERE CHARLES I SPENT HIS LAST NIGHT AS A FREE MAN IN 1646

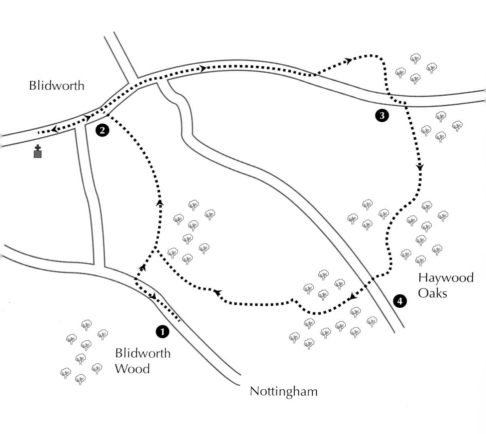

Blidworth

Blidworth
Wood

Haywood
Oaks

Nottingham

1 **2** **3** **4**

Blidworth and Haywood Oaks

6

LENGTH:	6 miles (9.7 km)
TIME:	3 hours
TERRAIN:	A stretch of road walking (mainly in Blidworth village) but mostly along forest tracks; one easy climb
START/PARKING:	Forestry Commission car park at Blidworth Wood; from the A614 between Nottingham and Ollerton take Blidworth Lane (signposted to Kirkby-in-Ashfield), GR SK595544
PUBLIC TRANSPORT:	None
REFRESHMENTS:	Pub near the start, pubs at Blidworth
MAP:	OS Explorer 270 – Sherwood Forest

The hilltop village of Blidworth was situated in the heart of medieval Sherwood and is not surprisingly associated with the Robin Hood legends. The surrounding area is still heavily wooded, even though many of the trees are more recent conifer plantings, but at one point the route passes the Haywood Oaks, survivals of the older forest. A lengthy but easy climb at the start brings you to Blidworth, where a brief diversion is made in order to visit the church. This is followed by a walk through the village and most of the return leg is through thick woodlands. From the higher points there are attractive and extensive views over fields and forest. Because of the absence of waymarking in much of the Forestry Commission woodlands, it is important to heed the route directions carefully, especially in the vicinity of the Haywood Oaks.

ⓘ The woods around Blidworth were mainly planted by the Forestry Commission in the years between the First and Second World Wars. Although chiefly comprising pines, there are also areas of open heath and some native broadleaved trees. Nowadays these woods are popular and attractive recreation areas for walkers, cyclists and horse riders.

❶ Begin by turning left out of the car park along the lane and after ¼ mile (400 m), turn right at a byway sign along an enclosed track (Beck Lane). There are fine all-round views as the track climbs steadily, eventually emerging at the top onto a road in Blidworth. Keep ahead to the main street.

ABOVE: BECK LANE, AN ENCLOSED TRACK THAT LEADS UP TO THE HILLTOP
VILLAGE OF BLIDWORTH

☈ ❷ **Turn left, still continuing uphill, for a detour to the church, situated at the highest point in the village.**

❶ All that remains of the medieval church at Blidworth is the fifteenth-century tower; the rest dates from an eighteenth-century rebuilding. Blidworth Church has a number of links with Sherwood Forest and the medieval outlaws, including a monument of a forest ranger, killed in Sherwood in the sixteenth century. In the churchyard there is also the alleged grave of Will Scarlet, one of the principal members of Robin Hood's outlaw band, believed to be situated somewhere near a group of yew trees and a fragment of the original church tower. Other legends suggest that Maid Marian may have lived in the village but, as with most of the Robin Hood stories, there is absolutely no evidence of this.

ABOVE: BLIDWORTH'S EIGHTEENTH-CENTURY CHURCH

Retrace your steps and continue down the steep main street to a road junction at the bottom. The lower part of Blidworth developed as a mining village in the 1920s but the mine closed in 1989.

At the junction turn right, in the Sherwood Forest direction, and just beyond the Jolly Friar Pub, bear left beside a gate – there is a Robin Hood Way sign here – and walk along a track. At a junction, keep along the right-hand one of two parallel tracks, which bends right and heads gently uphill to a road. Turn left to the Forestry Commission's Haywood Oaks car park.

❸ Turn right along a track. Pass beside a barrier and follow the track along the right edge of the trees. The curving track later enters woodland and after bending to the left on the edge of the trees, continues in a straight line.

Look out for any obvious paths on the right and take the second of these paths – there is a crossways here and the path is very sandy, almost like walking along a stretch of beach. The path leads you to the Haywood Oaks.

The Haywood Oaks are a remnant of ancient Sherwood that managed to survive the earlier destruction of so many other oak trees. They make an impressive sight, standing like sentinels amidst the more recent conifers.

Continue on the path beyond the line of old oaks, bending left to emerge onto a lane.

❹ Cross over to a barrier, pass beside it and walk along the straight, wooded track ahead. At a fork continue along the right-hand main track which curves right and at the next fork, the main track curves left and continues in a straight line.

At a junction turn right, shortly afterwards bend left, and at the next fork where the main track bends right, take the narrower path which runs along the left inside edge of the wood. Follow the edge of the trees first to the right and then to the left to emerge onto a track. This is Beck Lane where you should turn left, here picking up the outward route, and retrace your steps to the start.

OPPOSITE: A TRACK THROUGH BLIDWORTH WOOD

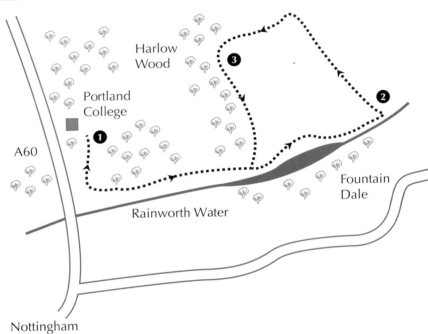

Mansfield

Harlow
Wood

3

2

Portland
College

1

A60

Fountain
Dale

Rainworth Water

Nottingham

Harlow Wood and Fountain Dale

7

LENGTH:	4 miles (6.4 km)
TIME:	2 hours
TERRAIN:	Some field paths but most of the route is along clear forest tracks
START/PARKING:	Portland College, off the A60 about 2 ½ miles to the south of Mansfield, GR SK551568
PUBLIC TRANSPORT:	Buses from Nottingham and Mansfield
REFRESHMENTS:	Café at Portland College
MAP:	OS Explorer 270 – Sherwood Forest

Most of this highly attractive walk is either through or along the edge of Harlow Wood. From Portland College a clear and easy path leads into Fountain Dale, the legendary home of Friar Tuck and the scene of the first meeting between the friar and Robin Hood. A gentle climb out of the dale across more open country is followed by a descent along the edge of the wood and a return to the start.

🛈 Portland College is a training college for the physically disabled and is named after Winifred Duchess of Portland who was one of the major driving forces behind its foundation in 1950. Initially it was intended to deal with members of the armed forces injured in war and for miners injured in mining accidents. The college is situated on the edge of Harlow Wood, has a café, gift shop and free car park. It also stands at the hub of many good paths through the forest.

❶ The walk begins in the visitors' car park. Look out for a gap in the railings on the west (main road) side of the car park, descend steps to a red-waymarked post and turn left along a path which leads into Harlow Wood.

Follow the clear, main path all the while, eventually emerging from thick woodland into more open country. At a crossways where there is a blue-waymarked fingerpost, keep ahead and shortly you will reach an arch-shaped information board about Fountain Dale, one of a series of 'In the Footsteps of Robin Hood' boards scattered throughout Sherwood.

❶ Fountain Dale is famed in the outlaw legends as the place where Robin Hood first met Friar Tuck. The friar is alleged to have lived here as a hermit and Friar Tuck's Well is named on Ordnance

ABOVE: IN HARLOW WOOD

Survey maps but the actual site is almost impossible to find amidst the thick vegetation of the dale.

The story about the first eventful meeting between the two men is told on the information board. According to the legends, Robin Hood was walking through the area and ordered the portly friar to carry him across the stream. Friar Tuck refused but, after being threatened with an arrow in his ribs, he reluctantly agreed. However, on the other side he turned the tables and demanded that Robin Hood should carry him back. A fight developed during which both ended up in the water, but as a result the two men developed a mutual respect, became firm friends for life and Friar Tuck joined the outlaw band. Like almost everything to do with Robin Hood, it is a great story and adds to the overall enjoyment of this walk, but as the character of Friar Tuck only appears in the later ballads, it has absolutely no factual foundation.

Beyond this information board the path curves right through Fountain Dale to reach a footbridge over a stream and marshy ground, passing to the left of an expanse of water. This is about the closest you can get to the alleged site of Friar Tuck's Well and it may have been around here that the apparent fight took place.

Continue along the right edge of a field, by woodland on the right, and look out for a yellow-topped post on the right. ❷ At this point turn left along a track through a young plantation to the far left-hand corner of the field, bear right and continue gently uphill along a narrow, enclosed path.

On emerging onto a track at the top of the rise, turn left, passing to the left of farm buildings, and follow an enclosed, tree-lined path to a crossways.

❸ Turn left along a track which descends gently along the left inside edge of Harlow Wood – a very attractive part of the walk – to a crossways at the bottom. Turn right, here joining the outward route, and retrace your steps to the start.

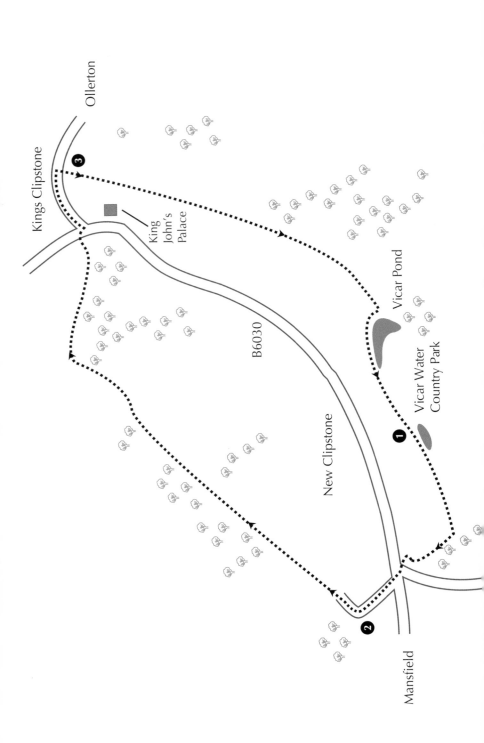

Vicar Water and Kings Clipstone

8

LENGTH:	5 ½ miles (8.9 km)
TIME:	3 hours
TERRAIN:	Clear and easy paths and tracks
START/PARKING:	Vicar Water Country Park, signposted from the B6030 at New Clipstone, GR SK587626
PUBLIC TRANSPORT:	Buses from Mansfield, Ollerton and Edwinstowe
REFRESHMENTS:	Café at Country Park, pub at Kings Clipstone
MAP:	OS Explorer 270 – Sherwood Forest

After a short stroll through the country park, head gently uphill above the village of New Clipstone and continue along a straight track above the Maun Valley for about 1 ¾ miles (2.8 km). Although only at a modest height, there are grand and extensive views from the track over the surrounding landscape of Sherwood Forest. An equally gentle descent brings you into Kings Clipstone where you can view – at a distance – the scanty remains of King John's Palace, a royal hunting lodge that has had quite a colourful history and is one of the few tangible links with the medieval forest. The final stretch is through the valley of the little River Maun, re-entering the country park. For much of the way the views are dominated by the headstocks of the former Clipstone Colliery, the tallest in Europe, as much a part of the history of this area of Sherwood as the palace ruins.

① The landscape around Vicar Water Country Park and Clipstone has almost turned full circle. Originally it was an area of rough forest and heath and Vicar Pond was created in 1870 as a fishery for the Duke of Portland. After the sinking of Clipstone Colliery in 1912, the pond was used by the local miners and soldiers from a nearby army camp for swimming and boating, and the land adjacent to it became a dumping ground for colliery waste. Reclamation began in 1982 with the opening of the country park and the colliery finally ceased production in 2003. Since then much of the land has reverted to grassland and wood; Vicar Pond is again used primarily for fishing and the whole area has regained its former tranquillity and is now used for recreational pursuits, chiefly cycling and walking.

❶ Facing the visitor centre, turn right and walk across the car park to a track by the end of a lake. Turn right along it, pass beside a barrier to leave the country park and keep

ABOVE: FROM CLIPSTONE DRIVE THERE ARE FINE VIEWS OVER SHERWOOD FOREST

OPPOSITE: THE SPARSE REMAINS OF KING JOHN'S PALACE, CLIPSTONE

ahead along a path. Immediately after passing Bridleways Holiday Homes and Guest House, turn right along a straight wide track.

Just before reaching a road, follow the track around a right bend and turn left through a gap to emerge onto the road. Cross over and take the road opposite (Newlands Drive), heading gently uphill.

❷ At a T-junction at the top, turn right into Clipstone Drive and where the road ends, keep ahead along a straight, enclosed track. Keep along this track for the next 1 ¾ miles (2.8 km) to where it broadens out in front of stable buildings and becomes a tarmac track. Follow it around a right bend and keep ahead into Kings Clipstone. At a T-junction bear right up to the main road and turn left, in the Ollerton direction.

❸ At a public bridleway sign in front of the Dog and Duck, turn right through the pub car park to information boards. These tell you about King John's Palace, the ruins of which can be seen on the skyline to the right.

❶ These meagre and rather forlorn looking remains – which can only be seen at a distance from over a fence – are of King John's Palace, a royal hunting lodge in the heart of Sherwood built in the twelfth century, not by King John, as the name implies, but by his father, Henry II. The palace was enlarged in the thirteenth century by Henry III and Edward I and was

at its height in the late twelfth, thirteenth and fourteenth centuries when it was visited frequently by successive medieval monarchs, as they could hunt in the forest without the lengthy journey from the royal castle at Nottingham. During this period several events of national importance occurred within the walls of these now scanty ruins. In 1194 after his return from the Holy Land, Richard I journeyed to Nottingham where the castle was in the hands of rebels in the service of his treacherous brother Prince John, one of the chief villains of the Robin Hood legends. After successfully recapturing the castle, historical documents record that the king 'set out to see Clipstone and the forest of Sherwood ... and they pleased him much'. While there he mixed business with pleasure by holding a summit meeting with the King of Scotland. When Edward I was staying here in 1290, he is reputed to have held a meeting of Parliament either at the palace or under a nearby oak tree, hence its name the Parliament Oak. In the later Middle Ages the popularity of the hunting lodge declined and by the end of the fifteenth century it had already fallen into ruin. The plundering of its stones over the following centuries has reduced it to its present state.

Continue along the path ahead through the valley of the narrow River Maun, going through a succession of gates. Shortly after passing under two disused railway bridges, you re-enter the country park and reach a T-junction in front of Vicar Pond. Turn right, follow the curve of the pond to the left and the path returns you to the start.

OPPOSITE: VICAR WATER COUNTRY PARK

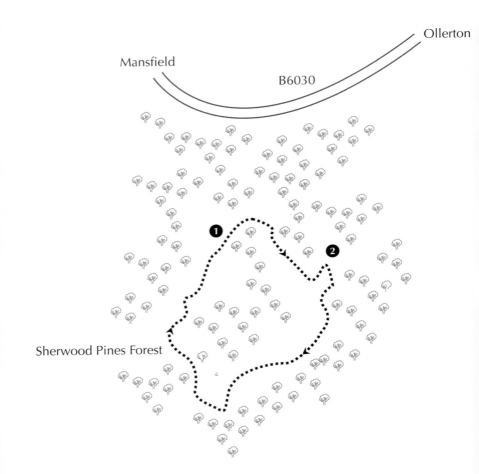

Sherwood Pines
Forest Park

LENGTH:	2 ½ miles (4 km)
TIME:	1 ½ hours
TERRAIN:	Gently undulating and well-waymarked forest paths and tracks
START/PARKING:	Sherwood Pines Forest Park, signposted from the B6030 between Ollerton and Clipstone, GR SK613636
PUBLIC TRANSPORT:	Buses from Mansfield, Ollerton and Edwinstowe to the park entrance, then a walk of just over ½ mile (800 m) to the start
REFRESHMENTS:	Café at the visitor centre
MAP:	OS Explorer 270 – Sherwood Forest

This walk introduces you to the more recent face of Sherwood Forest. As its name suggests, it takes you through some of the pine woodlands planted by the Forestry Commission in the 1920s on land that had in the past been part of the traditional forest landscape of oak, beech, birch and heath. It is a highly attractive walk with fine views, open grassland areas and remnants of the old forest as well as impressive stands of tall pines. Although the walk is fairly tortuous, it is easy to follow as you simply look out for the frequent blue-ringed and later blue- and white-ringed marker posts. It is also a well designed walking trail as it takes you through some of the older parts of the forest and for the most part it keeps away from the many cycle routes throughout the park.

ⓘ In the years following the end of World War I, the Forestry
Commission began the large-scale planting of conifer woodlands
in many parts of the old Sherwood Forest that had become
denuded of trees. One of the largest blocks was Clipstone Forest
which has now become the Sherwood Pines Forest Park. The
park, which covers an area of 3,300 acres, is accessible to the
public for the enjoyment of a wide variety of outdoor pursuits.
There are walking and cycling trails, children's play areas, treetop
adventures, horse riding facilities and opportunities to observe
wildlife. There is also a café. The forest park is ideal for a family
outing and although conifer woodlands, mainly of pine, inevitably
predominate, there are also areas of older broadleaved trees and
some open expanses of grassland and heath, as this walk reveals.

❶ **The walk begins in front of the café. With your back to
it, turn left along a track to the start of the blue trail and
continue along it, looking out for a blue-ringed post which
directs you to turn right onto a woodland path.**

**Follow the winding path gently downhill, cross a track
and keep ahead through an area of open heathland before
re-entering thick woodland. Turn left along an avenue of
older trees, turn right at a crossways – there are fine views
over to the left – and shortly after turn right again. The path
curves left, descends gently and then bends right.**

**After passing through a more open area, bear right along
a track and look out for where a post indicates a left turn
onto a narrower path. The path twists and turns to reach
a T-junction where you turn left, now following blue- and
white-ringed posts for the rest of the walk. Again the
path winds around to reach another T-junction in front of
Childhood Wood.**

ⓘ Ahead are a number of interpretation boards explaining the
inspiration behind the planting of Childhood Wood. The wood
was created in 1993 as a way of commemorating the lives of

OPPOSITE: ATTRACTIVE WOODLAND TRACK IN SHERWOOD PINES FOREST PARK

children that have been lost to a degenerative disease called mucopolysaccharide (MPS) for which there is no cure. It comprises young oak saplings that have been cloned from some of the ancient Sherwood oaks, part of the Forestry Commission's long term plans to restore the traditional oak and birch woodland to this part of Sherwood.

ABOVE: THERE ARE AREAS OF OPEN HEATHLAND AS WELL AS THICK WOODLAND IN THE FOREST PARK

❷ At the T-junction turn right beside the wood and head gently uphill to another T-junction. Turn right, not along the broad track but onto a parallel path, heading gently downhill, curving first right and then bending sharply to the left. Continue along another winding path to a T-junction, turn left to a track, cross over and keep ahead across open grassland to another T-junction.

Turn right to a crossways where a notice indicates the end of the blue and white trails that you have been following. From here turn left along a track which winds along the left edge of woodland to return to the start.

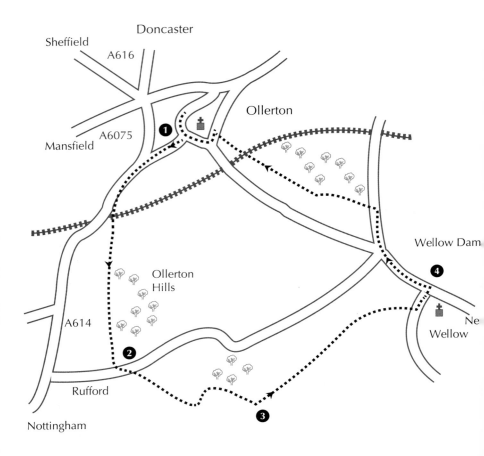

Ollerton, Rufford and Wellow

LENGTH:	**5 miles (8 km)**
TIME:	**2 ½ hours**
TERRAIN:	**Mainly on tracks and paths across fields and along the edge of woodland; some of the narrower paths may become overgrown during the summer**
START/PARKING:	**Ollerton, road junction in the village centre by the Hop Pole Hotel and Watermill, GR SK654675**
PUBLIC TRANSPORT:	**Buses from Nottingham, Worksop, Newark and Mansfield**
REFRESHMENTS:	**Pubs and café at Ollerton, café at Rufford Mill, pubs at Wellow**
MAP:	**OS Explorer 270 – Sherwood Forest**

This attractive and varied walk on the eastern fringes of Sherwood Forest falls naturally into three parts. On the first leg an easy and clear track leads from Ollerton to the edge of Rufford Abbey Country Park; next comes a stretch along tracks and across fields to the village of Wellow and on this part of the route there are wide views over the surrounding gently undulating countryside looking towards the forest. The last part of the walk from Wellow back to Ollerton is mainly along the edge of wooded slopes.

ⓘ Ollerton has always been an important route centre, located at a junction of two ancient routeways through Sherwood Forest: from Nottingham to Doncaster and Mansfield to Newark. In the Middle Ages it lay on the fringes of Sherwood; the River Maun which meets Rainworth Water here marked the eastern boundary of the forest. Despite being near a busy road junction and adjacent to a larger twentieth-century neighbouring town, the attractive old village, with its inns, cottages, watermill (now tea room) and eighteenth-century church, retains an old fashioned appearance and atmosphere and manages to remain an oasis of peace and tranquility.

❶ **Start by facing the watermill and turn left, in the Wellow and Newark direction. Opposite the church turn right along Station Road and bear left on reaching the A614. This is a busy road but the walk beside it is only ¼ mile (400 m) long and there is a pavement.**

Immediately after passing under a railway bridge, bear left along a track, at a public bridleway sign to Rufford. The track heads gently uphill, skirts the edge of the wooded Ollerton Hills and continues to a lane at Rufford. Just ahead is the country park and if you want refreshments, keep ahead into the park and turn right by the end of the lake to Rufford Mill.

ABOVE: APPROACHING RUFFORD

OPPOSITE: THE TRACK SKIRTS THE WOODED OLLERTON HILLS

ⓘ *For details of Rufford Abbey Country Park refer to Walk 13*

❷ **The route continues to the left along the lane. At the entrance to Rufford Park Golf and Country Club, bear right over a stile, at a public footpath sign, and walk along the tarmac track to Rufford Hills Farm.**

Where the track bears slightly left towards the farm, bear right across some grass to a stile. Climb it, keep ahead to climb another one and continue by the left edge of a field. At a hedge corner, follow the edge to the left and climb a stile in the corner of the field onto a tarmac track. Turn right and at a fork, take the straight, right-hand track which heads gently uphill.

❸ **Look out for a fingerpost at a junction of paths and tracks and turn left onto a narrow path. This path, which may get overgrown in the summer months, heads in a fairly straight line across a succession of fields – make sure that you keep ahead at all crossways and junctions – eventually reaching the top of a flight of steps above a former railway cutting.**

Descend the steps, cross a plank footbridge in the bottom of the cutting, ascend a similar flight of steps on the other side

**and keep ahead to a stile. After climbing it, continue along
the right edge of a series of fields, climbing a succession of
stiles.**

**In the corner of the last field – a sports field – turn
right along a track, go through a gate and keep ahead to
emerge onto a road in the village of Wellow. Turn left and
walk across the spacious and attractive village green to a
T-junction.**

ⓘ Cottages and inns line the wide expanse of the village green at
Wellow. Dominating the scene is the maypole, over 60 feet high,
which has been in existence for over 150 years. Every year on
the last Monday in May the village is a colourful sight when the
Wellow May Queen is crowned, an event followed by dancing
around the maypole and general festivities. In 1860 festivities got
rather out of hand when the pole was sawn down during drunken
revelries! Just off the green is the sturdy-looking medieval church,
much restored by the Victorians, and nearby is Wellow Dam, a
popular fishing and recreational area.

ABOVE: WELLOW CHURCH STANDS JUST OFF THE VILLAGE GREEN

OPPOSITE: WIDE VIEWS FROM THE PATH BETWEEN RUFFORD AND WELLOW

In the footsteps of Robin Hood   63

❹ Turn left along the main road, follow it around a right bend – Wellow Dam is over to the right – and where it curves left, turn right along a road signposted to Boughton and Retford.

Shortly after passing under a disused railway bridge where the road curves right, turn left, at a public footpath sign to Ollerton, along a narrow, enclosed path. Keep along the left edge of sloping woodland, follow the path around a left bend and at a fingerpost, turn right. Continue below sloping woodland on the right and on approaching a chalet park, go round right and left bends and the path emerges onto a tarmac drive.

Turn right over a railway bridge and then turn left – still by woodland on the right – into Ollerton. On reaching a road turn left, turn right at a sign for Ollerton Village and follow the road back to the start.

ABOVE: WELLOW DAM

OPPOSITE: OLLERTON'S EIGHTEENTH-CENTURY CHURCH

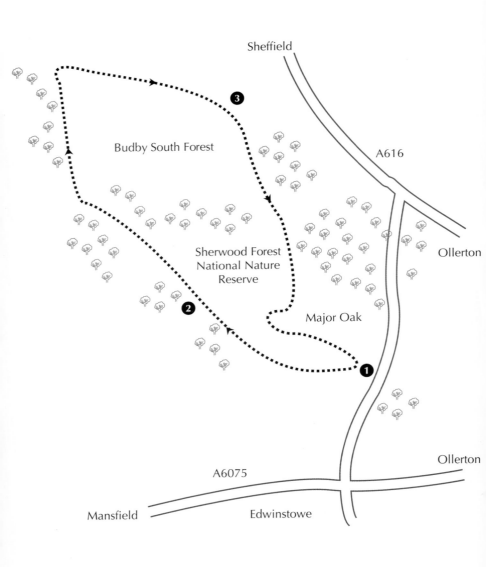

Birklands and the Major Oak

LENGTH:	4 ½ miles (7.2 km)
TIME:	2 hours
TERRAIN:	Clear tracks and paths through woodland and across heath
START/PARKING:	Sherwood Forest National Nature Reserve, off the B6034 ½ mile north of Edwinstowe village, GR SK626676
PUBLIC TRANSPORT:	Buses from Nottingham, Mansfield, Worksop and Ollerton (some seasonal) to Edwinstowe, from there a ½ mile (800 m) walk to the start. Also the Sherwood Forester bus service runs to the visitor centre from Nottingham and Worksop on Sundays and Bank Holiday Mondays from the beginning of May to the end of September, and some Sherwood Arrow buses run to the visitor centre from Nottingham and Worksop every day from the end of April to the end of September and on Sundays and Bank Holidays throughout the year.
REFRESHMENTS:	Café at visitor centre, pubs and cafés at nearby Edwinstowe
MAP:	OS Explorer 270 – Sherwood Forest

This walk takes you through the finest and most unchanged part of Sherwood Forest, the landscape of the traditional English greenwood and the part of modern Sherwood that would be most recognisable to Robin Hood. This is a walk where you can really let your imagination run riot and almost imagine outlaws in Lincoln Green lurking behind some of the massive trees or horsemen galloping along the forest paths. The first and last parts are through the glorious oak and birch woodland of Birklands and the middle section is across open heathland, as much a part of the medieval forest as the thick woodland. Towards the end you pass Sherwood's most visited and spectacular attraction, the mighty Major Oak.

❶ Sherwood Forest National Nature Reserve is based on the finest surviving part of old Sherwood. This is an area known as Birklands, so called because of the masses of silver birches that grow there, although it is the great oaks that tend to attract the most attention. Many of the gnarled old oaks are dying and their bare branches rising above the lower foliage give them the appearance of the antlers of a stag, hence their nickname stag-headed oaks. Some of their shapes are grotesque and can look quite terrifying, resembling prehistoric monsters or futuristic sculptures.

❶ It is worth spending some time at the visitor centre either at the start or finish of the walk. As well as the usual amenities – shop, restaurant, tourist information, books and leaflets – there is a fascinating and comprehensive exhibition about the forest and the legend of Robin Hood.

❶ The walk starts at the entrance to the visitor centre. Facing the entrance, turn left and at a fork immediately ahead, take the left-hand path. This path is signed Birklands Ramble and is initially waymarked with red-topped posts.

At a crossways keep ahead – there is a public bridleway sign – and at a fork a few yards in front, continue along the right-hand path, still following the red-topped posts.

❷ After descending to the next junction of paths in a slight dip, take the right-hand path, here leaving the red route and now following yellow waymarks. Keep ahead at a crossways – there is a public bridleway sign just in front – and the path eventually reaches a crossways and public bridleway sign just beyond a barrier.

Turn right along a track and after nearly ¾ mile (1.2 km), turn sharp right, in the Budby and Edwinstowe direction,

ABOVE: SOME OF THE ANCIENT GNARLED OAKS IN BIRKLANDS LOOK LIKE MONSTERS

OPPOSITE: ROBIN HOOD AND LITTLE JOHN, SHERWOOD FOREST VISITOR CENTRE

to enter the Dukeries Training Area. This is sometimes still used by the army for tank training and other exercises and you are warned not to stray from the paths or pick up any objects you might find. After ¾ mile (1.2 km) you reach a junction of tracks with two metal gates on the right and a kissing gate in between them.

❸ Go through the far gate and at a fork immediately ahead, continue along the left-hand grassy path across the open heathland of Budby South Forest.

❶ Budby South Forest has also now been included within the Sherwood Forest National Nature Reserve. It is a rare example of the open, sandy heathland that was found throughout the

ABOVE: ROUGH HEATHLAND IN BUDBY SOUTH FOREST

OPPOSITE: A TYPICAL SCENE IN BIRKLANDS, THE LANDSCAPE OF THE TRADITIONAL ENGLISH GREENWOOD

medieval forest and makes a striking contrast with the thick woodlands of Birklands. As in the past, it is still used for the grazing of sheep and cattle.

After crossing a track, the path re-enters the oak and birch woodland of Birklands. Pass beside a barrier, keep ahead to a crossways and turn right, in the Major Oak direction. The path curves left to the great tree.

Almost everyone who comes to Sherwood makes the short journey from the visitor centre to gaze at the Major Oak and the well-surfaced path is wheelchair and pushchair friendly. It is difficult to determine its age but it is many hundreds of years old, though perhaps not as old as the Robin Hood legends. Despite this, generations of children have been told that this is the tree in which Robin Hood used to hide from the Sheriff of Nottingham, and why not? It is a good story and makes the visit more enjoyable and in any case, the outlaw leader probably did hide in a tree that looked very similar!

Contrary to popular belief, the tree gets its name not from its size but from a Major Rooke who first described it in a book in 1799. Previously it had been called the Queen Oak and at one time the Cock Pen Tree on account of it being used as a venue for cockfighting. Since the early nineteenth century it has been a popular tourist attraction, particularly after the coming of the railway to Edwinstowe when visitors used to journey here from the station in horse-drawn carriages and picnic under its branches. It is certainly an impressive sight but well past its sell-by date and, like an elderly or infirm relative, it has to be propped up by various supports. At one time you could go right up to it and climb in the trunk but the passage of feet was compacting the soil, starving the tree of water and slowly killing the roots. Since it was fenced off, a green sward has grown up

ABOVE: ANCIENT OAKS LINE THE PATH THROUGH BIRKLANDS

OPPOSITE: THE MAJOR OAK, MONARCH OF THE FOREST

around it which has helped to bring about a recovery. It still looks healthy, produces a good crop of leaves and hopefully, despite its advanced age, there is still plenty of life left in this monarch of the forest.

Continue along the path which leads back to the start, a distance of about ½ mile (800 m).

In the footsteps of Robin Hood   73

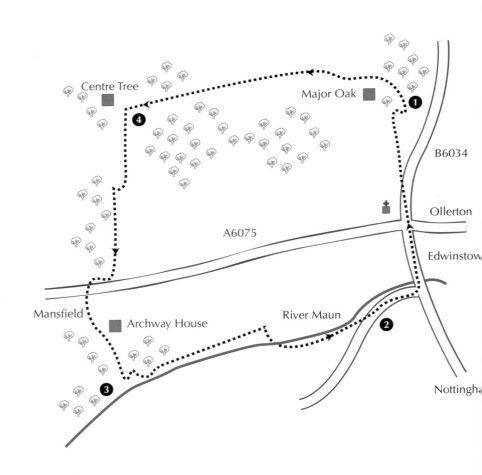

Centre Tree

Major Oak

❶

❹

B6034

Ollerton

A6075

Edwinstow

Mansfield

Archway House

River Maun

❷

Nottingh.

❸

Edwinstowe, River Maun and Birklands

12

LENGTH:	5 miles (8 km)
TIME:	2 ½ hours
TERRAIN:	Easy, well-signed field and forest paths and tracks
START/PARKING:	Sherwood Forest National Nature Reserve, off the B6034 ½ mile north of Edwinstowe village, GR SK626676
PUBLIC TRANSPORT:	Buses from Nottingham, Mansfield, Worksop and Ollerton (some seasonal) to Edwinstowe, from there a ½ mile (800 m) walk to the start. Also the Sherwood Forester bus service runs to the visitor centre from Nottingham and Worksop on Sundays and Bank Holiday Mondays from the beginning of May to the end of September, and some Sherwood Arrow buses run to the visitor centre from Nottingham and Worksop every day from the end of April to the end of September and on Sundays and Bank Holidays throughout the year.
REFRESHMENTS:	Café at the visitor centre, pubs and cafés at Edwinstowe
MAP:	OS Explorer 270 – Sherwood Forest

There is a strong Robin Hood theme throughout this walk. Like the last walk it begins at the Sherwood Forest National Nature Reserve and the first and last parts of the route are through the oak and birch

ABOVE: ANCIENT OAKS IN BIRKLANDS

OPPOSITE: EDWINSTOWE'S PICTURESQUE CRICKET GROUND, ON THE
EDGE OF THE FOREST

woods of Birklands, the finest surviving part of medieval Sherwood and the part that would be most recognisable to Robin and his men today. In between you walk through the village of Edwinstowe, passing the church in which, according to legend, Robin Hood and Maid Marian were married, and stroll through more open country along the pleasant banks of the River Maun. Re-entering Birklands, you come to the Centre Tree, one of the forest's great oaks and a major landmark, and towards the end you pass the mighty Major Oak, undoubtedly Sherwood's best known and most visited attraction.

ℹ️ *For details on Birklands and the Sherwood Forest National Nature Reserve refer to the previous walk*

❶ **The walk starts at the entrance to the visitor centre. Facing the entrance turn left and at a fork ahead, take the left-hand path, signed Birklands Ramble. At the first crossways turn left, immediately keep along the right-hand path at a fork and head gently downhill to a gate.**

Go through to emerge from the trees and, skirting the edge of Edwinstowe cricket ground, keep ahead to a road.

In the footsteps of Robin Hood   77

Continue into Edwinstowe to a crossroads, passing to the left of St Mary's Church.

ℹ️ Edwinstowe describes itself as Robin Hood's Village and it certainly has many connections with the forest and its outlaws. For a start it is situated in the heart of Sherwood and right on the doorstep of its finest remaining woodlands. In the Middle Ages it was one of the meeting places for the Forest Courts. And of course its thirteenth-century parish church is the alleged setting for the marriage of Robin and Maid Marian. As usual there is not a scrap of factual evidence for this, but it is a good story in a most appropriate venue and makes a visit to the church that much more enjoyable.

🚶 **At the crossroads keep ahead down High Street, looking out for a sculpture of Robin and Marian on the right, and shortly after crossing a bridge over the River Maun, turn right along Mill Lane.**

OPPOSITE: EDWINSTOWE CHURCH

ABOVE: INFORMATION BOARD IN THE CHURCHYARD AT EDWINSTOWE

❷ Just before reaching a railway bridge, turn right, at a public bridleway sign, and walk along the right edge of a field. The River Maun is just below on the right. Continue along an enclosed path, turn right to cross a footbridge over the river, keep along the right field edge to a T-junction and turn left below an embankment.

Later continue along the right inside edge of woodland and after emerging from the trees, keep ahead beside the river to a T-junction.

❸ Turn right gently uphill along a hedge-lined track, re-entering woodland, to reach Archway House.

❶ If you have already done Walk 18 you may notice that this is almost identical to the gatehouse of Worksop Priory, except that it has statues of the Sherwood outlaws rather than kings and saints. In fact it is a copy of the priory gatehouse, built in 1844 by the 4th Duke of Portland to sit astride a wide, straight drive that he planned to construct through the forest from his residence at Welbeck Abbey to Nottingham, a distance of over 20 miles. Not surprisingly this project, ambitious even by Victorian standards, was never realised. Archway House is now a private residence but can be clearly seen from the track.

Keep along a tarmac track to a road, cross over to footpath and cycleway signs opposite and turn right along a woodland path parallel to the road. At a crossways, turn left along a

straight track and after it broadens out, look out for a post and path on the right.

Walk along the path to a fingerpost ahead and turn left along a track parallel to the previous one to reach a crossways at the Centre Tree, a large and well-proportioned oak that marks the centre of the forest. It does not matter if you fail to spot the path on the right as the first track also leads to the Centre Tree.

🧍 **❹** Turn right, pass beside a barrier and continue along a straight track through the oaks and silver birches of Birklands. Keep in a straight line at all path junctions, following Robin Hood Way signs, eventually reaching a T-junction, and turn right to the Major Oak.

❶ *For details on the Major Oak refer to the previous walk*

🧍 Continue along the broad path which curves slightly left to return to the start, a distance of about ½ mile (800 m).

ABOVE: THE MAJOR OAK, MOST POPULAR SPOT IN SHERWOOD

OPPOSITE: RIVER MAUN

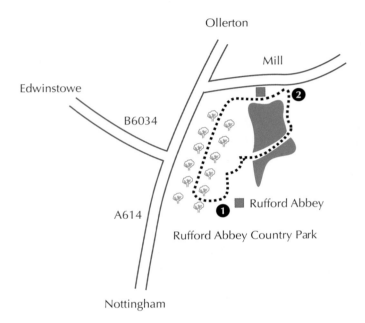

Ollerton

Mill

Edwinstowe

B6034

A614

Nottingham

2

1

■ Rufford Abbey

Rufford Abbey Country Park

Rufford: Abbey, Mill and Park

LENGTH:	2 miles (3.2 km)
TIME:	1 hour
TERRAIN:	Easy paths and tracks through woodland, across parkland and beside a lake
START/PARKING:	Rufford Abbey Country Park, off A614, 2 miles south of Ollerton, GR SK644647
PUBLIC TRANSPORT:	Buses from Nottingham, Edwinstowe and Worksop
REFRESHMENTS:	Cafés at Rufford Abbey, café at Rufford Mill
MAP:	OS Explorer 270 – Sherwood Forest

Rufford Abbey Country Park is based on the grounds that surrounded what was once a great country house, and for a short walk there is an incredible amount of variety: woodland, landscaped parkland, lake, craft centre, former mill buildings, the ruined house on the site of a former monastery and animal graves. The route is well-signed, easy to follow and provides a series of splendid views, especially across the lake. There is also the opportunity at the end to explore the formal gardens near the house.

❶ Rufford Abbey has certainly had a chequered history. A Cistercian monastery was founded here on the edge of Sherwood Forest in 1147. After a fairly uneventful history, it suffered the same fate as all the other English monasteries and was closed down by Henry VIII in the 1530s. The monastic lands were subsequently bought by the Earls of Shrewsbury, who built a house on the site. In 1626 the estate came into the possession of the Savile family who were to be the owners of Rufford for the next 300 years.

They made changes and additions to the house and carried out improvements to the grounds. Landscaping of the park took place in the seventeenth and eighteenth centuries and the lake was built around 1750.

The heyday of Rufford Abbey was the Victorian and Edwardian era during which a frequent visitor was the Prince of Wales, later Edward VII. He came here for shooting expeditions and also used the house as a convenient place to stay when visiting Doncaster races. The good times came to an end after World War I and in 1931 the estate was sold and broken up. The army took it over during World War II – it housed Italian prisoners of war – but after the war it was abandoned and neglected. In the early 1950s the house and some of the grounds were bought by Nottinghamshire County Council but the house was in such a bad condition that repair would have been too expensive and therefore the decision was taken to demolish it. As a result all that remains is part of the original sixteenth-century building which protected what was left of the medieval abbey.

Rufford's revival began in 1969 with the creation of the country park. The remains – both of the Cistercian abbey and the

house – were renovated and made safe, the grounds were tidied up and restored to much of their former splendour and the formal gardens were recreated. From a dilapidated ruin surrounded by a neglected and overgrown park, the place was transformed into the present attractive and popular amenity.

❶ Start in front of the ruined house and with your back to the entrance, walk along the main drive (Lime Tree Avenue) towards the main road. At a crossways, turn right along a track which passes along the left edge of a car park, and at a junction keep ahead into the lovely woodland of The Wilderness to the Ice House. This is where food for the great house was stored to keep it cool and fresh in the days before refrigeration.

Continue through the trees to a car park and in front of the Lakeside Garden Shop, turn right to a T-junction in front of Rufford Lake. Turn left onto a lakeside tarmac path and to the left are the buildings of Rufford Mill.

Above and opposite: the remains of Rufford Abbey, a country house on the site of a medieval abbey

ℹ️ After restoration, the buildings of the former corn mill and sawmill were converted into a tea room, outdoor shop and venue for conferences, weddings and other events.

🚶 **Continue past the mill and cross a footbridge at the corner of the lake.**

🚶 **❷ At a T-junction, turn right along a tree-shaded path, still beside the lake, and the path descends gently and bends right to cross a footbridge. Continue along a winding path, crossing a series of footbridges, and at a junction of paths keep ahead, in the Broad Ride and Animal Graves direction. Turn left, passing to the left of the animal graves.**

ℹ️ Most of the graves are those of dogs that were the pets of the Savile family. The largest one is that of the famous racehorse Cremorne, owned by Henry Savile and winner of the 1872 Derby.

🚶 **Turn right at a T-junction and opposite the Broad Ride, turn left onto a path signed Craft Centre. At the next T-junction turn right and go up some steps. The path bends left and leads back to the start.**

ABOVE AND OPPOSITE: IDYLLIC VIEWS ACROSS RUFFORD LAKE

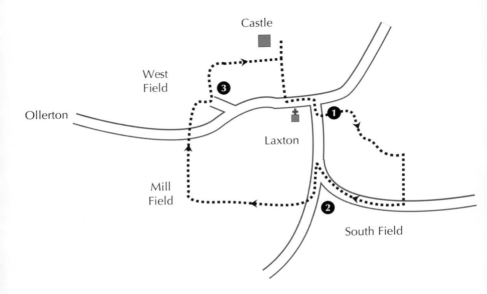

Castle

West
Field

3

Ollerton

Laxton

1

Mill
Field

2

South Field

Laxton and its Open Fields

14

LENGTH:	3 ½ miles (5.6 km)
TIME:	2 hours
TERRAIN:	Mostly well-signed field paths and tracks, a few muddy and overgrown stretches likely
START/PARKING:	Laxton, situated on a side road between the A6075 and A616 about 5 miles to the east of Ollerton, GR SK724672. Car park behind the Dovecote Inn
PUBLIC TRANSPORT:	Buses from Ollerton and Retford
REFRESHMENTS:	Pub at Laxton
MAP:	OS Explorer 271 – Newark-on-Trent

For much of the Middle Ages Laxton Castle was the seat of power of the chief foresters of Sherwood, the king's principal agents and law enforcers in the royal forest. Nowadays this small hilltop village, situated amidst pleasant rolling countryside to the east of Sherwood Forest, is famous for being the only place in England where the ancient open field system of farming is still practised. The walk takes you across some of the open fields where information boards give full details of how the system operates. More information on the history of Laxton and why and how the open field system has survived here can be found in the visitor centre at the start of the walk.

ℹ️ A visit to Laxton enables you to get an insight into a way of life that was common throughout England during the Middle Ages, which had started to decline by the Tudor period and had virtually vanished by the early nineteenth century. Uniquely it has survived in this small, off the beaten track, Nottinghamshire village a few miles to the east of Sherwood Forest.

The open field system operated on a communal basis. Each farmer had strips of land in each of the large fields around the village and the crops were grown on a rotation system. The usual rotation was on a three-year cycle: wheat was grown for one year, barley or oats for another year and during the third year the field was left fallow; i.e. it was rested in order for the soil to regain its goodness. Such a system was wasteful because of the unused land that separated each of the strips, and inefficient because it was difficult to keep weeds in check and also did not allow for experimentation. Between the sixteenth and nineteenth centuries the open fields were gradually converted into consolidated blocks of enclosed fields farmed individually, which enabled greater productivity, improved methods of farming and more flexible rotations and varieties of crops. Three of the original four open fields still remain at Laxton – South Field, Mill Field and West Field – and why and how they have survived at all is remarkable. The traditional rotation of crops is still used but obviously requires a high degree of co-operation amongst the participating farmers.

It is interesting to note that in Laxton many of the old cottages were formerly farms because under the open field system it was normal for the farmers to live in the local village as it was usually in the middle of the communal fields. It was only after the change to farming in compact, individual, enclosed fields that it became more convenient to live in farm houses close to those fields.

❶ Turn left out of the car park down Main Street, passing the old pinfold on the left, and at a public footpath sign, turn left over a stile onto a narrow, enclosed path. Climb a stile, head uphill along the right field edge to climb another one and continue along the enclosed path. Turn right over a stile, turn left along a field edge and go through a gap in the hedge to a crossways and fingerpost.

Turn right along the right edge of the next two fields, climbing a stile, and in the corner of the second field go through a kissing gate. Now continue along the left edge of a succession of fields, going through a series of kissing gates.

After the fourth kissing gate, turn left along the left edge of a field, go through another kissing gate and keep ahead

ABOVE: GENTLY ROLLING NOTTINGHAMSHIRE COUNTRYSIDE NEAR LAXTON

OPPOSITE: ONE OF A NUMBER OF INFORMATION BOARDS IN THE OPEN FIELDS AROUND LAXTON

across the next field to a yellow-topped post and public footpath sign. Turn right along a sunken track, go through a kissing gate, continue along a track and go through a gate onto a lane.

Turn right – South Field is over to the left – and the lane curves right back towards Laxton. At a road junction on the edge of the village, turn sharp left along Kneesall Road.

❷ After ¼ mile (400 m), turn right through a gate, at a public footpath sign, and keep ahead, by a hedge on the left, up to another gate. Go through it, continue gently uphill through a narrow belt of woodland, later keeping along the right edge of the trees and then along a track by a left field edge.

At a fingerpost by a hedge corner keep ahead across Mill Field to a crossways where there is an information board. Turn right along a stony track continuing across the field to a road. Cross over and take the gently ascending concessionary track ahead, later continuing along a narrow, sunken path to a T-junction. Turn right back towards the village.

ABOVE: MILL FIELD, ONE OF THE THREE REMAINING OPEN FIELDS

OPPOSITE: THE CHURCH AT LAXTON

❸ On emerging onto a track, turn left. This is also a concessionary route. Just before the track curves left, bear right by a hedge on the right to an information board about West Field and turn right over a stile.

Walk along the field edge, keep ahead over a stile and continue along an enclosed path to a T-junction. Just to the left a kissing gate admits you to the earthworks of Laxton Castle.

ℹ All that is left of the castle is the motte, or mound, and associated earthworks. It was the stronghold of the Caux and Everingham families who for much of the Middle Ages were the hereditary stewards or chief foresters of Sherwood. Their function was to uphold the forest laws on behalf of the king, including bringing outlaws to justice. Laxton's handsome medieval church, which you pass shortly, contains tombs of some of the Everinghams. The church was heavily restored and partially rebuilt in the Victorian era when the nave was shortened and the distinctive pinnacles and pyramid-shaped spire added to the tower.

The route continues to the right along a wide, hedge-lined track to emerge onto a road opposite Laxton Church. Turn left to return to the start.

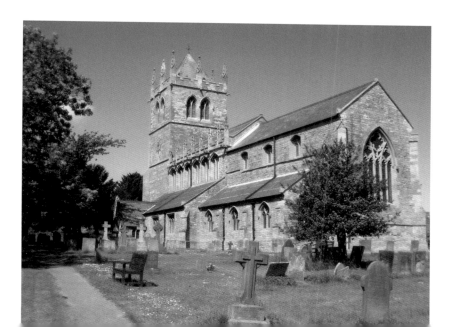

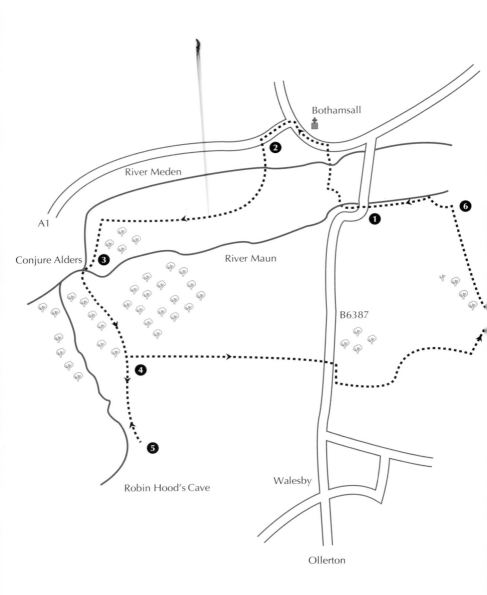

Conjure Alders and Robin Hood's Cave

LENGTH:	7 miles (11.3 km)
TIME:	3 ½ hours
TERRAIN:	Clear and easy paths and tracks across fields and through woodland
START/PARKING:	Small car park on the B6387 ¾ mile south of Bothamsall, GR SK681686
PUBLIC TRANSPORT:	None to the start, but buses to Bothamsall from Ollerton and Retford
REFRESHMENTS:	None
MAP:	OS Explorer 270 – Sherwood Forest

The rivers Meden and Maun feature prominently throughout this walk, especially in the woodland of Conjure Alders which was the north-eastern corner of Sherwood Forest in medieval times. Here the two rivers briefly join and then separate again to continue on their individual courses. There is much attractive woodland, pleasant walking by the rivers, wide views across the Nottinghamshire countryside and a brief and very worthwhile detour to a cave associated with Robin Hood. From here you enjoy the finest view on the route.

❶ Turn left out of the car park along the road and at a public footpath sign, turn right through a kissing gate. Walk through an area of widely spaced trees, cross a footbridge over the River Maun and keep ahead in the direction of Bothamsall Church seen on the horizon.

Bear right to cross a footbridge over a ditch, keep ahead to cross another footbridge over the River Meden and continue along a path to emerge onto a road. Turn left uphill into the village of Bothamsall and follow the road around a left bend by the nineteenth-century church.

❷ At a public footpath sign, turn left onto a gently descending track. The track becomes enclosed and on emerging into open country, there is a good view to the right of the motte, or mound, of what was a Norman castle on the site of an earlier earthwork.

Recross the River Meden, keep ahead and the track curves right and then right again to continue first between fields and later along the right edge of woodland. At the corner of the trees, turn left and the route continues between woodland on the left and the Meden on the right to where it meets the River Maun.

❶ The adjacent woodland of Conjure Alders was the north-eastern corner of the medieval royal forest of Sherwood and gets its name from the large number of alder trees. Alders like damp conditions and flourish here in the marshy ground near the rivers. The Maun and Meden briefly join here then separate after about 200 yards (183 m) – at the point where the Maun bends left – to continue on their respective ways. The Maun, which the route follows for the next mile (1.6 km), marked the eastern boundary of Sherwood Forest.

❸ Keep ahead over a footbridge, turn right beside the combined rivers, ignore another footbridge on the right and keep ahead, curving gradually left through woodland. Continue gently uphill to a junction and keep ahead to a meeting of paths on the edge of the trees by a yellow-topped post.

ABOVE: CONJURE ALDERS, AN IDYLLIC SPOT ON THE EASTERN FRINGES OF SHERWOOD FOREST WHERE THE RIVERS MEDEN AND MAUN BRIEFLY JOIN

OPPOSITE: EARTHWORKS OF THE FORMER CASTLE AT BOTHAMSALL

❹ Turn left here to continue on the main route but keep ahead for the short detour to Robin Hood's Cave, just over ¾ mile (1.2 km) along a tree-lined track which climbs gently to a sandstone outcrop from where there is a fine view over the Maun Valley.

ⓘ The caves below the outcrop are one of many sites scattered throughout Sherwood and beyond that claim to be one of the places where the outlaw leader sought refuge from his enemies. It is worth the detour as it makes a good resting place from which you can enjoy the magnificent view, looking across the Maun Valley towards the thick woodlands of Thoresby and Clumber on the horizon.

❺ Retrace your steps to the path junction on the edge of the woodland ❹ and turn right to keep along the right inside edge of the trees.

After crossing a bridge over a disused railway track, the route continues along a narrower path to a road. Cross over,

ABOVE AND OPPOSITE: LOOKING ACROSS THE MAUN VALLEY FROM THE SPLENDID VIEWPOINT OF ROBIN HOOD'S CAVE

immediately turn right along the right edge of a field and in
the corner turn left to continue along the right field edge.
Go through a gap in the next corner, turn left along a track,
follow it around a right bend and in the corner of the field,
turn left and continue along the right edge of the field.

Where the field ends, keep ahead along a narrower path
to a T-junction, turn left along a track and follow it around
a right bend. The track becomes hedge-lined, then passes
through woodland and later continues across fields to a
T-junction.

❻ Turn left, follow the track around a right bend and at a
fingerpost in front of a gate, turn left along the right field
edge. Go through a hedge gap, keep along the right edge of
the next field – the River Maun is on the right – pass under
a disused railway bridge and the path ahead leads back to
the car park.

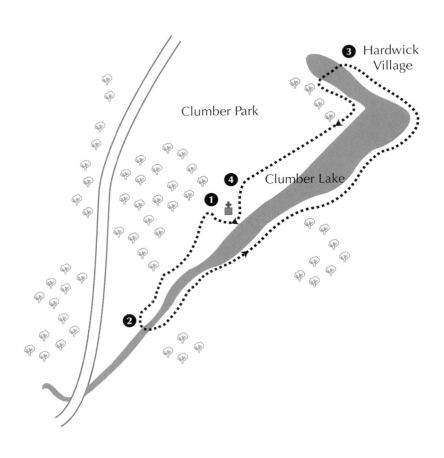

3 Hardwick Village

Clumber Park

Clumber Lake

4

1

2

Clumber Park: Around the Lake

16

LENGTH:	4 miles (6.4 km)
TIME:	2 hours
TERRAIN:	Flat tracks and paths through woodland, across grassland and beside the lake
START/PARKING:	Clumber Park, accessed either from the A614 to the east or the B6034 to the west between Ollerton and Worksop, GR SK625746
PUBLIC TRANSPORT:	Some Sherwood Forester buses from Worksop and Nottingham at weekends and Bank Holidays during the summer months
REFRESHMENTS:	Café at Clumber Park
MAP:	OS Explorer 270 – Sherwood Forest

As one of Sherwood Forest's most popular attractions and also one of the National Trust's major flagships, Clumber Park merits two walks. This one is basically a circuit of Clumber Lake, sometimes by the edge of the water and at other times further away through woodland. On the middle section of the route along the southern shore of the lake, the extensive views over the parkland and across the water to the church are especially memorable.

ⓘ Clumber Park was originally an area of rough woodland and
heath on the northern fringes of Sherwood Forest. An early
eighteenth-century visitor was obviously not impressed, describing
it as 'a black heath full of rabbits, having a narrow river running
through it, with a small boggy close or two'. In 1707 it was
enclosed from the forest by the Duke of Newcastle as a hunting
park for Queen Anne. Around the middle of the eighteenth
century the landscaping of the park was begun by Stephen
Wright and continued after his death by John Simpson. Between
them they created this superb parkland with sweeping grassland,
extensive woodland (retaining many of the ancient trees of the
forest), a serpentine lake created by damming the little River
Poulter, imitation Greek and Roman temples and an elegant
Classical bridge. Landscaped gardens, new plantings of trees and
grand avenues were added in the nineteenth century.

ABOVE: THE MAGNIFICENT VIEW ACROSS THE LAKE TO CLUMBER CHURCH

At the centre of it all stood a grand eighteenth-century house which became the main residence of the Dukes of Newcastle. The house was largely destroyed by a disastrous fire in 1879 but in its place a huge Italian-style mansion, designed by Charles Barry, was built. Of this house virtually nothing survives, not because of a later fire or neglect but by taxation and the rising costs of its upkeep. The family decided to abandon it, the contents were auctioned off and in 1938 the house was so thoroughly demolished that only a small corner of it (formerly the duke's study) survives, plus the original stable block. These buildings are used by the National Trust as offices, shop, information centre and café.

Fortunately the beautiful Victorian church remains and of course the great park. After being requisitioned by the War Department during World War II, the park was purchased by the National Trust in 1946 and over the past half-century the Trust has done much to restore it to its original glory. Now the beauty of this former private estate can be enjoyed by all, with miles of tarmac drives and grassy woodland tracks to explore, either on foot or bicycle.

ABOVE: CLUMBER CHURCH AND LAKE

❶ The walk starts at the car park by the main visitor amenities. Turn right out of the car park along a tarmac drive, using the path on the left parallel to it.

Keep along this path to join another stretch of tarmac drive, looking out for the directions to Lakeside, follow the drive to the right and just before reaching a vehicle barrier, turn left off it onto a path through woodland.

Pass a grotto, which used to be part of the water supply to the estate, and continue through the trees to emerge onto a tarmac drive just to the right of Clumber Bridge.

❷ Turn left to cross the bridge, pausing to admire the view, and turn left along a lakeside path. After passing through

ABOVE: THE ELEGANT EIGHTEENTH-CENTURY BRIDGE OVER THE END OF THE
LAKE AT CLUMBER PARK

a car park, the route continues along the south side of the lake, sometimes through woodland and sometimes across open grassland, with superb views all the way.

At the far end of the lake, the path – now on an embankment – follows the curve of the lake to the left, keeping to the left of the estate village of Hardwick. Pass through a car park and on joining a tarmac drive, bear left along it.

❸ Cross a causeway over an arm of the lake, at a fork take the left-hand track and on the other side, turn left onto a path through trees parallel with the water. The path follows the curve of the lake to the right and continues through the beautiful Ash Tree Hill Wood to a T-junction.

Turn left along a path which bends right in front of the gates of the Pleasure Ground and continue along the fence-lined path between open grassland on the right and woodland on the left.

ABOVE: THIS FRAGMENT IS ALL THAT IS LEFT OF THE GREAT HOUSE OF THE DUKES OF NEWCASTLE

❹ Just before reaching a tarmac drive, turn left, in the Pleasure Ground direction, go through a gate, and walk along a winding path through trees to a crossways.

ⓘ The Pleasure Ground was laid out in the eighteenth century and comprises around 24 acres of trees and shrubs interspersed with grassy glades, an ideal spot for a relaxing stroll. To the right is the church, whose elegant tower and spire have been in sight throughout much of the walk. It was built in 1889 as a private chapel for the family and their tenants and estate workers by the 7th Duke of Newcastle, and it stands in an idyllic position near the lake and site of the former house. Of almost cathedral-like proportions, it is regarded as an outstanding example of Victorian architecture.

Turn right towards the church, keep to the right of it and at a T-junction, turn left to pass in front of it. The path curves left to pass in front of what is left of Clumber House and curves right into the courtyard. Keep ahead past the stable block and on between buildings to return to the start.

Opposite: stable block at Clumber

Above: track through Ash Tree Hill Wood at Clumber

In the footsteps of Robin Hood   107

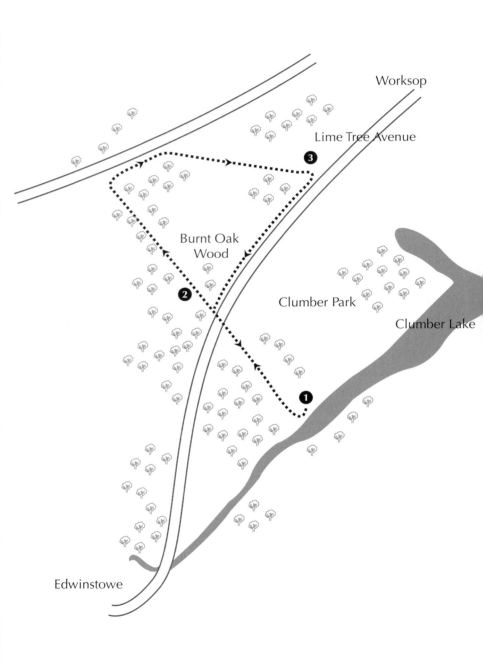

Worksop

Lime Tree Avenue

❸

Burnt Oak
Wood

Clumber Park

Clumber Lake

❷

❶

Edwinstowe

Clumber Park: Lime Tree Avenue

17

LENGTH:	4 miles (6.4 km)
TIME:	2 hours
TERRAIN:	Mainly along clear and flat woodland paths and tracks
START/PARKING:	Clumber Park, accessed from either the A614 to the east or the B6034 to the west between Ollerton and Worksop, GR SK625746
PUBLIC TRANSPORT:	Some Sherwood Forester buses from Worksop and Nottingham at weekends and Bank Holidays during the summer months
REFRESHMENTS:	Café at Clumber Park
MAP:	OS Explorer 270 – Sherwood Forest

The second of the two walks through the extensive parkland of Clumber takes you away from the house, church and lake to the northern part of Clumber. There is much attractive woodland walking and the highlight is undoubtedly a walk along part of the magnificent Lime Tree Avenue, or Duke's Drive, allegedly the longest drive in Europe.

ⓘ *For details on Clumber refer to the previous walk*

❶ The walk starts at the car park by the main visitor amenities. Turn right out of the car park along a tarmac drive and at a junction, turn right along another tarmac drive. Soon after passing a pay booth, you reach a crossroads at the end of the Lime Tree Avenue. Cross over and continue along a tarmac drive.

❷ About 100 yards (91 m) further on, bear right along a straight path through Burnt Oak Wood. After nearly ¾ mile (1.2 km) where blue waymarks indicate a turn to the left, keep ahead, passing under a red and white archway and beside a barrier, and continue to a lane. Turn right and after ¼ mile (400 m), take the first track on the right. Keep

ABOVE: WOODLAND AND GRASSLAND AT CLUMBER

OPPOSITE: THE IMPRESSIVE LIME TREE AVENUE AT CLUMBER, ALMOST 3 MILES LONG

in a straight line along the main track all the while, finally emerging into a more open area. A few yards ahead is the Lime Tree Avenue.

ℹ The Lime Tree Avenue, or Duke's Drive, is a magnificent sight, approached from Apley Head Lodge entrance off the A614. The curving drive is just under 3 miles (4.8 km) long and consists of four avenues of lime trees, two each side of the drive, each tree the same height and equidistant from its neighbour. It comprises 1,296 trees and was planted in the middle of the nineteenth century by the 5th Duke of Newcastle. As the longest front drive in Europe, it remains one of the most striking examples of the wealth, power, style and supreme self-confidence of the Victorian aristocracy during the heyday of the country estate.

❸ Turn right along a path parallel to the drive as far as a crossroads. Turn left, here picking up the outward route and retrace your steps to the start.

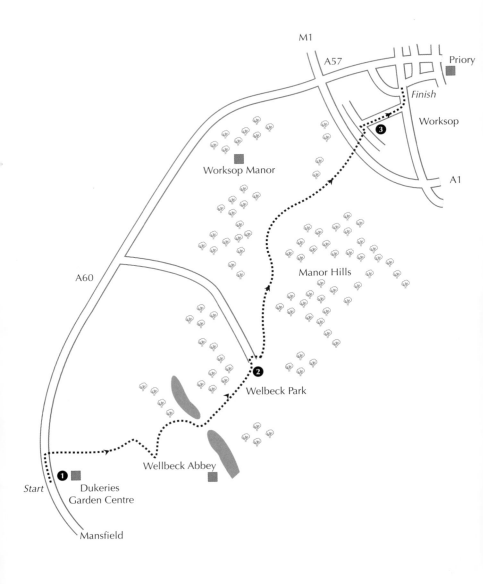

M1

A57

Priory

Finish

Worksop

3

Worksop Manor

A1

Manor Hills

A60

2

Welbeck Park

Wellbeck Abbey

Start

1 Dukeries
Garden Centre

Mansfield

Welbeck Park and Worksop

18

LENGTH:	5 miles (8 km)
TIME:	2 ½ hours
TERRAIN:	Easy and clear paths and tracks through woodland and across fields
START/PARKING:	Welbeck, Dukeries Garden Centre, on the A60 about 3 ½ miles south of Worksop, GR SK546742. Park at Worksop and catch bus 9 from Hardy Street to the start (contact Veolia Transport for information on bus times at 08700 121212 or www.veolia-transport.co.uk)
FINISH:	Worksop, Market Place, GR SK585786
PUBLIC TRANSPORT:	Buses from Mansfield, Doncaster and Chesterfield
REFRESHMENTS:	Cafés at the Dukeries Garden Centre and adjacent Harley Gallery, pubs and cafés at Worksop
MAP:	OS Explorer 270 – Sherwood Forest

This is a linear walk on the northern edge of Sherwood Forest and after arriving at Worksop you begin with a 10 minute bus journey, getting off at the entrance to the Dukeries Garden Centre. The walk back to Worksop takes you across part of Welbeck Park, one of the great estates of the Dukeries, and over the gentle wooded slopes of the Manor Hills, the latter a glorious sight in spring when they are carpeted with bluebells. Along the way there are wide views over

the surrounding countryside and reminders of the eccentricities of a nineteenth-century Duke of Portland, owner of the Welbeck estate.

❶ Facing the entrance to the Dukeries Garden Centre, turn right along the road (there is a pavement on the left side). After about ¼ mile (400 m) – at a public footpath sign on the left – turn right, pass beside a barrier and walk along a tree-lined tarmac track, joining the Robin Hood Way.

Keep ahead at a crossways and follow the winding track across fields, keeping ahead at another crossways and curving right towards the edge of woodland. At a public bridleway sign turn left along a grassy path which keeps along the left edge of the trees, later curving slightly right and continuing through the woodland.

Turn right on reaching a tree-lined tarmac track and at a fingerpost in front of one of the gates to Welbeck Abbey,

ABOVE: IN WELBECK PARK

turn left along a path which crosses a causeway between two lakes and continues across fields.

ℹ Welbeck Abbey overlooks the lake on the right but cannot be seen from the public footpath. The great house, which mainly dates from the nineteenth century, occupies the site of a medieval abbey. For many years it was the home of the Dukes of Portland and its heyday was towards the end of the nineteenth century and the early twentieth century when, under the 6th Duke, it was the venue for many glittering social occasions. The good times came to an end in the 1930s when the family moved out. During World War II Welbeck was taken over by the army and later used as a sixth form college for future officers. In 2005 the army relinquished it and its future is currently uncertain. It is a pity that the public cannot visit it as it would be one of the most interesting houses in the country, chiefly because of the activities of the eccentric 5th Duke of Portland who indulged in grandiose

ABOVE: VIEW OVER THE LAKE AT WELBECK

and highly expensive subterranean building projects, including tunnels and a huge ballroom. One of the tunnel entrances will be seen later.

🚶 **At a crossways keep ahead to a public footpath sign by a gate, go through, turn right alongside a fence, go through another gate and turn left, passing in front of a lodge to a T-junction. Turn left – here leaving the Robin Hood Way – and on the left is one of the Welbeck tunnel entrances.**

ℹ The tunnel entrance is the clue to the strange personality of the 5th Duke of Portland who, as already mentioned, built many underground rooms at Welbeck Abbey. The reason for his mania for building underground is that he was an exceptionally shy, although a kindly and philanthropic man, who disliked being seen and lived as a virtual recluse in just a few rooms of the great

ABOVE: ENTRANCE TO THE UNDERGROUND TUNNELS AT WELBECK

OPPOSITE: DISTANT VIEW OF WORKSOP MANOR

house. The tunnels were built in order that when he had to go to London, he could travel unseen in his carriage from the house to the edge of the estate and then on to Worksop railway station. There the carriage would be loaded onto a railway truck, enabling him to travel the rest of the way in complete privacy.

❷ **At a public footpath sign to Worksop, turn right through a gate. Keep ahead along a path and on joining a track, continue along it over the gentle wooded slopes of the Manor Hills, arguably the most attractive part of the walk. After emerging from the trees, keep initially along the right edge of fields and later along an enclosed track. Ahead Worksop Manor can be seen.**

ⓘ At one time Worksop Manor belonged to the Dukes of Norfolk and if the grandiose ambitions of the 9th Duke had ever been fully realised, it would have been one of the largest palaces in Europe. Only the north wing was ever built and when the house was sold to the Duke of Newcastle in 1840, he had no need for such a large house so near his main residence at Clumber. Therefore much of it was dismantled and converted into the present private residence.

(🚶) Continue ahead at a junction of tracks but look out for where you bear right off the track to climb a stile. Walk along the right edge of fields and in the corner of the last field, climb a stile and keep ahead to another one. After climbing it, head up and down steps, carefully cross the busy A57 and repeat the up and down procedure on the other side. Follow the path first to the left and then to the right to emerge onto a track and turn left to a road on the edge of Worksop.

(🚶) ❸ Turn left, take the first road on the right (Robinson Drive) and follow it to the main road. Turn left along the road to the Market Place where the walk finishes.

🛈 Worksop lies on the northern fringes of Sherwood Forest and describes itself as 'The Gateway to the Dukeries.' In the Middle Ages it was a place of safety for travellers after the considerable dangers of journeying through the wild and outlaw-infested forest. It is best known for its Augustinian priory, founded in 1103 and dissolved by Henry VIII in 1539. After the dissolution, the land

ABOVE: WEST FRONT OF WORKSOP PRIORY

and buildings were granted to Francis Talbot, Earl of Shrewsbury on condition that he and his successors provided a glove for the right hand of monarchs at their coronation. This custom still survives. Over the following centuries the monastic buildings were demolished and their stone plundered, but the nave of the church survived as the local parish church. This dates from the twelfth century and is a particularly impressive example of Norman architecture. The destruction of the east end of the church left the thirteenth-century lady chapel isolated but a programme of restoration, which began in the nineteenth century and was completed in the 1970s, resulted in the building of a new east end and central tower which has restored unity to the church.

To the south of the church is the well-preserved fourteenth-century monastic gateway, the only other part of the medieval priory to survive. Its roof and doors are made from Sherwood oak, thought to have been part of a grant of 200 oak trees made to the Prior of Worksop in the early fourteenth century.

ABOVE: WORKSOP PRIORY FROM THE SOUTH

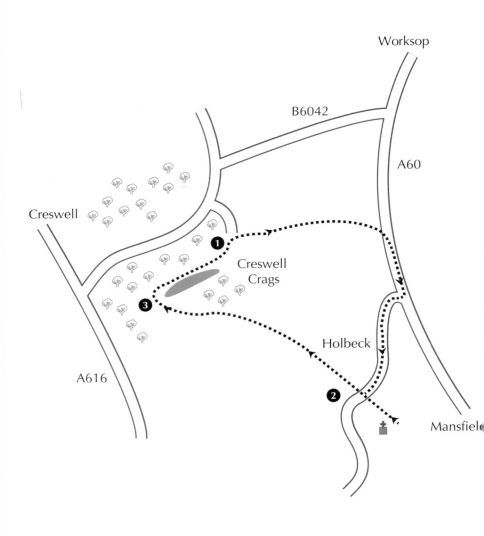

Creswell Crags and Holbeck

19

LENGTH:	3 miles (4.8 km)
TIME:	1 ½ hours
TERRAIN:	Mostly woodland tracks and field paths with a small amount of road walking
START/PARKING:	Creswell Crags, signposted from the A60 between Mansfield and Worksop, GR SK538745
PUBLIC TRANSPORT:	Buses from Mansfield and Worksop stop on the A60 from where you can join the walk soon after the start
REFRESHMENTS:	Café at the visitor centre, cafés at the Dukeries Garden Centre and adjacent Harley Gallery
MAP:	OS Explorer 270 – Sherwood Forest

Parts of this walk straddle the Nottinghamshire-Derbyshire border on the north-western fringes of Sherwood Forest. The first part of the route is along an attractive tree-lined track, followed by a short stretch of road walking. A quiet lane brings you into the tiny hamlet of Holbeck and from there field paths lead to the impressive limestone gorge of Creswell Crags. The final leg – and the undoubted highlight of the walk – is through this fascinating gorge, only about ½ mile (800 m) long but well worth taking plenty of time over. Although the walk starts by the visitor centre, it is recommended that you leave it until the end in order to appreciate the history and significance of the gorge and view some of the many items that have been found there. Besides you can always combine this with something to eat and drink.

❶ Start by walking to the far end of the car park, pass beside a barrier and take the straight, tree-lined track ahead. After ½ mile (800 m) you emerge onto the A60.

Turn right and soon after passing the entrance to the Harley Gallery and Dukeries Garden Centre, turn right along the lane signposted to Holbeck. Follow the lane around a left bend and continue into Holbeck, curving right through the hamlet.

❷ At a public footpath sign, turn left along a tree-lined track for a brief detour to St Winifred's Church.

ℹ This small church was built in 1913 to serve the family, tenants and estate workers of the Duke of Portland, and is situated on a small rise overlooking Welbeck Park. In the churchyard are the graves of many of the Portland family, some of whom were brought here from their original burial place at Welbeck Abbey after the church was built.

Retrace your steps along the track, turn left to continue briefly along the lane and at a public footpath sign, turn

ABOVE: TREE-LINED TRACK AT THE START OF THE WALK

OPPOSITE: CAVES AT CRESWELL CRAGS

right onto a track. Where the track bends right to a
gate, keep ahead along a rising path through trees to
emerge into a field.

Walk along the left edge of two fields, head across the
next field and after passing a redundant stile, continue
along the right field edge. In the next field continue
gently uphill along the right edge, follow the edge as it
bears left and go through a gap in the hedge at the top.

Ahead the scene is dominated by the village
of Creswell and the buildings of the
former colliery, but you are shortly
to enter a much different world,
the world of prehistory. Keep
ahead, descending quite
steeply, and the path bends
right and heads down to a
stone stile. Climb it and
continue down steps
into the gorge.

❸ Here you have a choice; either walk along the right edge of the gorge, keeping to the right of the lake, or along the left side, passing to the left of the lake. Better still, do a circuit of the gorge, a distance of only about ¾ mile (1.2 km), pausing to look at the information boards located at the entrances to many of the caves.

Afterwards, in order to return to the start, take the path signposted to the museum and car park at the far end of the lake. The path heads gently down through trees and then rises to a T-junction. The visitor centre and car park are to the right.

❶ The wooded limestone ravine of Creswell Crags, sometimes referred to as the 'Cheddar of the North', is renowned as one of the earliest known places of human habitation in Britain. Here during the last Ice Age, 50,000 to 10,000 years ago, roamed prehistoric man, and in the caves that line both sides of the gorge, archaeologists have discovered stone tools and the remains of beasts such as bison, mammoth and reindeer. In addition the only examples of prehistoric cave art in the country have been found here.

As these caves have been used for human habitation throughout the centuries, it is likely that among those seeking shelter and refuge were some of Sherwood's medieval outlaws, including Robin Hood and his men; one of them is called Robin Hood's Cave. In the visitor centre there are many exhibits and displays and it is possible to tour some of the caves.

OPPOSITE: CRESWELL CRAGS

ABOVE TOP: DID ROBIN HOOD SEEK REFUGE HERE?

ABOVE BOTTOM: THE SMALL, SECLUDED CHURCH AT HOLBECK

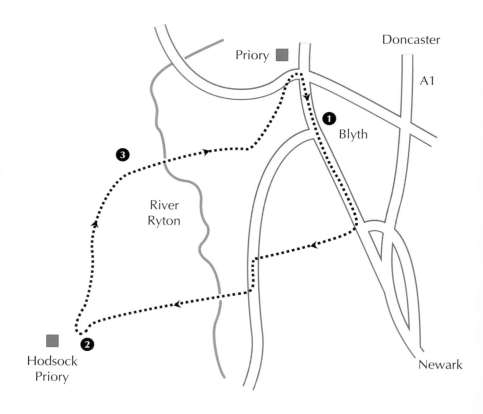

Doncaster

A1

Priory

Blyth

❶

River
Ryton

❸

❷

Hodsock
Priory

Newark

Blyth and Hodsock Priory

20

LENGTH:	3 ½ miles (5.6 km)
TIME:	2 hours
TERRAIN:	Flat and easy walking along tarmac drives and field paths
START/PARKING:	Blyth, parking spaces on High Street by the White Swan Pub, GR SK626868
PUBLIC TRANSPORT:	Buses from Worksop and Doncaster
REFRESHMENTS:	Pubs at Blyth
MAP:	OS Explorer 279 – Doncaster

Blyth is situated in the heart of Robin Hood country, roughly half-way between the forests of Sherwood and Barnsdale, the outlaw leader's principal haunts, close to the Nottinghamshire-South Yorkshire border. The terrain in this area is flat and open and throughout the walk there are extensive views across the surrounding countryside, with the tower of Blyth Priory prominent for much of the way.

❶ In the Middle Ages Blyth had strong links with Sherwood Forest and is mentioned in some of the early Robin Hood legends. It was situated on the main road between London and York, the chief routeway between Sherwood and Barnsdale, and had a priory that was regularly granted gifts of timber from Sherwood for building purposes. The priory was founded in 1088 by Roger de Busli, one of the Norman knights who helped William the Conqueror win the Battle of Hastings, and as a reward was given large estates in North Nottinghamshire and South Yorkshire. After the dissolution of the monasteries in the 1530s, the east end of

the church and all the monastic buildings were demolished and what is left today is the nave of the former priory church and a later western tower. The nave, built in the late eleventh century, is an outstanding example of early, plain Norman architecture

Blyth continued to be an important stopping place on the Great North Road until the building of a recent bypass, hence its wide High Street and large number of inns. At the south end of the large green is a restored building, originally dating from the twelfth century, which was once the leper hospital of St John the Evangelist.

❶ With your back to the White Swan, turn left along High Street and near the end of the wide green you pass the former hospital of St John the Evangelist. Follow the road out of the village and just before reaching a traffic island, turn right, at a public footpath sign, along the tarmac drive to Spital Farm.

Walk between the farm buildings and continue along the straight, tree-lined drive, descending gently to a road. Turn left and at a sign to Hodsock Priory, turn right along another

ABOVE: FORMER LEPER HOSPITAL AT BLYTH

OPPOSITE: GATEHOUSE OF HODSOCK PRIORY

straight, tarmac drive. **Cross a bridge over the little River Ryton and keep ahead towards the gatehouse of Hodsock Priory.**

❶ For about six weeks every year during February and March the gardens of Hodsock Priory are open to enable visitors to see the magnificent display of snowdrops. The house, which is not open to the public, mainly dates from the nineteenth century, with the Tudor gatehouse as an exception.

❷ Just before reaching the gatehouse, turn sharp right, at a waymarked post, along a fence-lined track to another waymarked post at the entrance to the next field. Bear right across the field, in the direction of the yellow waymark, and head gently uphill towards a fence corner on the right edge of a small clump of trees.

Continue past the trees along the left field edge to a stile. Climb it, bear right and keep in a straight line across the next three fields, going through a series of hedge gaps all clearly shown with yellow waymarked posts.

❸ After passing through the third hedge gap, turn right along the right field edge, keep ahead through a group of trees and recross the River Ryton via a footbridge.

Continue along a right field edge, go through a fence gap and bear slightly left to the next gap where a yellow waymark directs you to bear right along a track.

Head gently uphill along the left edge of a field to a T-junction and turn left along a tree-lined track to a road. Turn right back into Blyth and follow the road around a right bend to a T-junction. A path on the left leads to the priory; to return to the start turn right to the green at the top of High Street.

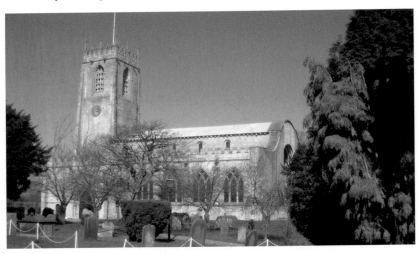

TOP: RIVER RYTON NEAR BLYTH

ABOVE: BLYTH PRIORY